Family Issues in the 21st Century

Temporary Assistance for Needy Families

Promising Employment Approaches and Program Provisions

FAMILY ISSUES IN THE 21ST CENTURY

Additional books in this series can be found on Nova's website under the Series tab.

Additional e-books in this series can be found on Nova's website under the e-book tab.

FAMILY ISSUES IN THE 21ST CENTURY

TEMPORARY ASSISTANCE FOR NEEDY FAMILIES

PROMISING EMPLOYMENT APPROACHES AND PROGRAM PROVISIONS

SALVATORE HOFFMAN
EDITOR

nova publishers
New York

Library of Congress Cataloging-in-Publication Data

ISBN: 978-1-63482-612-9

Published by Nova Science Publishers, Inc. † New York

CONTENTS

PREFACE

One of the central features of the Temporary Assistance for Needy Families (TANF) block grant is promoting work and job preparation for parents (mostly single mothers) in families that receive cash assistance. The TANF block grant requires states to engage a certain percentage of work-eligible cash assistance recipients in specified work-related activities, such as job search assistance and training. Yet, data suggest that more TANF recipients could receive assistance that would help them gain employment and reduce their dependence. This book reviews some approaches that have been identified as holding promise for engaging TANF recipients in employment and increasing their earnings and examines ways in which selected states and localities have used them; and identifies factors that influence their use.

Chapter 1 - The TANF block grant requires states to engage a certain percentage of work-eligible cash assistance recipients in specified work-related activities, such as job search assistance and training. Yet, data suggest that more TANF recipients could receive assistance that would help them gain employment and reduce their dependence. GAO was asked to provide examples of what some states are doing to achieve these goals and how to expand these efforts.

This report (1) reviews some approaches that have been identified as holding promise for engaging TANF recipients in employment and increasing their earnings and examines ways in which selected states and localities have used them, and (2) identifies factors that influence their use. To first identify promising approaches, GAO reviewed summaries and syntheses of rigorous research on approaches that increase employment and earnings, and profiled 10 state and local programs that were nominated by experts familiar with welfare research and state and local efforts, and that were selected to represent a range of approaches. GAO also reviewed relevant federal laws, regulations, and agency guidance, and interviewed agency officials and experts with a range of views.

Chapter 2 - One of the central features of the Temporary Assistance for Needy Families (TANF) block grant is promoting work and job preparation for parents (mostly single mothers) in families that receive cash assistance. TANF was created in the 1996 welfare law, which was the culmination of a decades-long evolution from providing single mothers "pensions" to permit them to stay home and raise children to a program focused on work. State TANF programs were influenced by research conducted during a period of much experimentation on welfare-to-work initiatives in the 1980s and early 1990s, which found that mandatory work requirements could reduce welfare receipt and increase employment among single mothers.

TANF aids some of the most disadvantaged families with children. These families are in a wide range of circumstances, and some of them are not subject to state welfare-to-work efforts. In FY2011, about 6 in 10 TANF assistance families had "work-eligible" individuals. TANF work-eligible individuals comprise in great part single mothers with young children. In FY2011, about a third of TANF work-eligible mothers were young (under the age of 24). Additionally, 40% of all work-eligible women lacked a high school diploma or the equivalent.

As a block grant to the states, TANF sets federal goals such as ending dependence of needy parents on government through work and job preparation, gives states flexibility in program design to achieve those goals, and measures the performance of states. The work requirements that actually apply to recipients are determined by the states, not by federal rules. In FY2011, 42% (monthly average) of all work-eligible adults were either working or engaged in a job preparation activity. The most common activity was working in a job while remaining on the rolls. Job search and vocational educational training followed as the second and third most common activities.

While state rules—not federal rules—determine work requirements for individual TANF recipients, federal TANF law establishes work participation standards that apply to the states and influence state program designs. The federal work standards are performance measures used to assess state TANF welfare-to-work efforts. The federal TANF work standards set target participation rates, specify activities that can be counted toward meeting the standards, and set minimum hours of engagement per week in a month for a recipient to be considered engaged in countable activities. The target participation rates vary by state: the statute sets a 50% standard for all families, but the standard is reduced by credits states may earn for caseload reduction. In FY2011, the official TANF work participation *rate* was 29.5%; however, all but seven states, the District of Columbia, and Guam met their all-family work *standard*.

The TANF work standards date back to the 1996 law, and reflect the policy concerns and the research on welfare-to-work programs of the time. Research on new welfare-to-work models since the 1996 law has yielded mixed and limited results. However, some innovations in workforce and education programs have yet to be tested within a welfare-to-work context. Policy makers also face questions about whether the sole focus of the assessment of TANF's success ought to be welfare-to-work. TANF has evolved into a program where cash assistance represents less than 30% of its funds. Policy makers thus face questions of whether consideration might be given to developing measures and assessment of how well TANF does in meeting other goals related to improving the circumstances of families with children.

In: Temporary Assistance for Needy Families ISBN: 978-1-63482-612-9
Editor: Salvatore Hoffman

Chapter 1

TEMPORARY ASSISTANCE FOR NEEDY FAMILIES: ACTION IS NEEDED TO BETTER PROMOTE EMPLOYMENT-FOCUSED APPROACHES*

United States Government Accountability Office

WHY GAO DID THIS STUDY

The TANF block grant requires states to engage a certain percentage of work-eligible cash assistance recipients in specified work-related activities, such as job search assistance and training. Yet, data suggest that more TANF recipients could receive assistance that would help them gain employment and reduce their dependence. GAO was asked to provide examples of what some states are doing to achieve these goals and how to expand these efforts.

This report (1) reviews some approaches that have been identified as holding promise for engaging TANF recipients in employment and increasing their earnings and examines ways in which selected states and localities have used them, and (2) identifies factors that influence their use. To first identify promising approaches, GAO reviewed summaries and syntheses of rigorous research on approaches that increase employment and earnings, and profiled

* This is an edited, reformatted and augmented version of a United States Government Accountability Office. publication, No. GAO-15-31, dated November 2014.

10 state and local programs that were nominated by experts familiar with welfare research and state and local efforts, and that were selected to represent a range of approaches. GAO also reviewed relevant federal laws, regulations, and agency guidance, and interviewed agency officials and experts with a range of views.

WHAT GAO RECOMMENDS

GAO recommends that HHS should issue guidance to clarify how the career pathways approach can be used by TANF agencies and identify potential changes to address the lack of incentives in the TANF program. HHS agreed with GAO's recommendations.

WHAT GAO FOUND

The 10 state and local programs GAO examined used various promising approaches to help Temporary Assistance for Needy Families (TANF) cash assistance recipients gain employment by meeting a range of participant needs. These approaches included the use of subsidized employment, employment alongside treatment for a health condition, and training for high-demand jobs. For example, for individuals in need of additional work experience, San Francisco's TANF program has provided subsidies to employers to place participants in temporary, wage-paying jobs. To help individuals with mental and physical disabilities and substance abuse problems, nonprofit contractors for New York City's TANF program have provided individualized assessment and treatment, often combined with employment. To prepare individuals with various skill levels for high-demand jobs, Minnesota and Washington have used a career pathways approach of combining occupation-specific training with basic skills education and support services. However, experts told us that some states have a misperception that this approach is not allowable under TANF rules, even though the Departments of Labor, Education, and Health and Human Services (HHS) support its use. HHS told us that states could still meet program requirements while using this approach, but the agency has not issued formal guidance clarifying this. Internal control standards for the federal government state that information should be communicated to managers in a form that enables them to carry out their responsibilities. As a result of these misperceptions, the career pathways approach may be underused by TANF agencies and TANF recipients could miss out on the potential benefits of this approach.

Expertise and dedicated funds facilitated use of these promising approaches, but the federal TANF program, itself, lacks incentives for their wider adoption. Of the 10 programs GAO examined, 9 drew on the expertise of partner organizations— including community college systems, workforce agencies, and nonprofits. The programs also benefitted from decisions by state and local policymakers to dedicate funds—including TANF funds—for the selected programs, according to officials. However, incentives for large numbers of state and local TANF agencies to adopt and test promising approaches are lacking under the structure of the TANF program for several reasons. First, many program design and funding choices are left to the states, and GAO's prior work has shown that state use of TANF funds for more costly welfare-to-work approaches can compete with other allowable uses of TANF funds. Second, TANF's main performance measure does not necessarily encourage agencies to use certain approaches that incorporate longer-term education and training or treatment services, although states are not prohibited from doing so. Third, little incentive exists for TANF agencies to evaluate their programs. HHS's authority over many aspects of TANF is limited and it has not proposed legislative changes to address these areas. Yet, because HHS oversees TANF, it is positioned to identify, suggest, and work in consultation with Congress on potential changes that would better address the lack of incentives for the use of promising approaches by states and to better meet the TANF goal of increasing employment. Without federal action, adoption and evaluation of promising approaches may continue to be limited to select states and localities, leaving TANF recipients in other locations without access to these promising approaches.

ABBREVIATIONS

AFDC	Aid to Families with Dependent Children
HHS	Department of Health and Human Services
MOE	maintenance of effort
PRWORA	Personal Responsibility and Work Opportunity Reconciliation Act of 1996
TANF	Temporary Assistance for Needy Families

November 19, 2014

The Honorable Orrin Hatch
Ranking Member
Committee on Finance
United States Senate

The Honorable Dave Reichert
Chairman
Subcommittee on Human Resources
Committee on Ways and Means
House of Representatives

The Temporary Assistance for Needy Families (TANF) block grant, administered by the U.S. Department of Health and Human Services (HHS), provides $16.5 billion annually in federal funding to states for cash assistance as well as a variety of other benefits and services to meet the needs of low-income families with children.[1] In March 2014, states used federal and state TANF funds to provide cash assistance to 1.6 million low-income families nationwide.[2] In keeping with a TANF goal of reducing families' dependence on government by promoting work, TANF requires states to engage a certain percentage of families with a work-eligible individual receiving cash assistance in specified work-related activities or face potential financial penalties. These work activities include, for example, unsubsidized employment, job search and job readiness assistance, certain training and education, and work experience. In recent years, some state TANF agencies have narrowed the scope of services they provide, reportedly in response to resource constraints and staff reductions. Related to this trend, data suggest that more TANF recipients—especially those considered hard to employ—could receive assistance that will help them to gain employment and reduce their dependence on cash assistance.

GAO has been asked to provide examples of what some states are doing now to help TANF recipients reach these goals and how these efforts can be expanded. Our report (1) reviews some approaches that have been identified as holding promise to engage TANF recipients in employment and increase their earnings and examines ways in which selected states and localities have used them, and (2) identifies factors that influence the use of these and other promising approaches.

To first identify promising approaches, we reviewed research summaries and syntheses of rigorous research on promising approaches for engaging TANF recipients in employment and increasing their earnings.[3] To identify state and local programs that are currently using these approaches to serve TANF cash assistance recipients, we interviewed cognizant researchers; officials from HHS, the Department of Labor, and the Department of Education; and others with TANF expertise. We selected 12 experts based on their knowledge of the research and efforts under way at the state and local level, as well as to reflect a range of perspectives on welfare-to-work issues. We identified them through our literature review and through referrals from other experts. We selected 10 programs to profile (located in 6 states—California, Kentucky, Minnesota, New York, Utah, and Washington—and the District of Columbia) from those nominated by experts to reflect diversity in approaches used, economic conditions, demographics, and geographic regions, among other factors. We conducted in-depth interviews, by phone and through four site visits, with program administrators and state and local TANF officials to learn about key program features that might increase employment and incomes. We obtained views from experts; federal, state, and local officials; and program administrators on factors that facilitate the use of promising approaches and that could broaden their use. We assessed information and communication HHS provides to states related to promising approaches against federal internal control standards.[4] We obtained budget, performance, and other program data for the programs we selected, and reviewed HHS administrative data on states' engagement of TANF recipients in prescribed work activities. We assessed the reliability of these data by reviewing related documentation and interviewing knowledgeable officials and determined they were sufficiently reliable for providing contextual information on these programs and describing work participation trends, respectively. We also reviewed relevant GAO, HHS Office of Inspector General, and HHS reports, as well as relevant federal laws, regulations, and guidance. Appendix I describes our objectives, scope, and methodology in greater detail.

We conducted this performance audit from January 2014 to November 2014 in accordance with generally accepted government auditing standards. Those standards require that we plan and perform the audit to obtain sufficient, appropriate evidence to provide a reasonable basis for our findings and conclusions based on our audit objectives. We believe that the evidence obtained provides a reasonable basis for our findings and conclusions based on our audit objectives.

BACKGROUND

TANF and the Work Participation Rate

The Personal Responsibility and Work Opportunity Reconciliation Act of 1996 (PRWORA) established four purposes for the TANF block grant:

1) provide assistance to needy families so that children may be cared for in their own homes or homes of relatives;
2) end dependence of needy parents on government benefits by promoting job preparation, work, and marriage;
3) prevent and reduce out-of-wedlock pregnancies; and
4) encourage two-parent families.[5]

Within these goals, states have responsibility for designing, implementing, and administering their welfare programs to comply with federal guidelines, as defined by federal law and HHS, including imposing a 5- year lifetime limit on many families receiving cash assistance.[6] In addition, the block grant includes a maintenance-of-effort (MOE) requirement, which requires states to maintain a significant portion of their historic financial commitment to welfare-related programs. In fiscal year 2013, states spent a total of $31.6 billion in federal TANF funds and state MOE funds, with federal funds accounting for 53 percent of the total. The federal law that established TANF also created a TANF Contingency Fund that states could access in times of economic distress.[7] In creating the TANF block grant, Congress emphasized the importance of state flexibility, and restricted HHS's regulatory authority over the states except to the extent expressly provided in the law.

In line with the second purpose, a key TANF goal is helping parents prepare for and find jobs. The primary means for measuring state efforts in this area has been TANF's work participation rate. Generally, states are held accountable for ensuring that at least 50 percent of all families receiving TANF cash assistance and considered work-eligible participate in one or more of the federally-defined allowable activities for the required number of hours each month.[8] The law also contains a provision known as the caseload reduction credit, which allows states to reduce the work participation rate they are required to meet based on reductions in the size of their TANF caseload.[9] In addition, TANF regulations provide that states that spend more than their MOE requirements generally receive an increase in their caseload reduction credit.[10]

TANF Programs Currently Engage Recipients in a Limited Range of Work-related Activities

Our work has shown that over the years, states have engaged about one third of families receiving TANF cash assistance in federally-defined work activities nationwide while still meeting their required work participation rates. Generally, this is because many states have relied on the caseload reduction credit and other allowable options to meet the requirement rather than engaging more families in specified work activities to reach a 50 percent rate. This has raised concerns among some policymakers that states are meeting the letter but not the spirit of the law. PRWORA established higher work participation rate requirements and eliminated many exemptions from these requirements for recipients compared to what was in place prior to TANF.[11] This reflected research that found that mandatory work requirements could reduce welfare receipt and increase employment among single mothers and help address concerns about long-term welfare receipt. In our prior work, we concluded that states' use of the modifications currently allowed in federal law and regulations, as well as states' policy choices, have diminished the usefulness of the work participation rate as a national TANF performance measure.[12]

The Claims Resolution Act of 2010 required states to report additional information on TANF recipients' engagement in activities.[13] An HHS report to Congress, based on 2011 state data, found that that 24 percent of work-eligible individuals met federal work participation rate standards, but more than 50 percent of work-eligible individuals had zero hours of participation (see fig. 1).[14] While some of these individuals were exempted from participation or excluded for some other reason such as caring for a child under age one, at least some of these individuals had not been engaged in work activities by the state or local TANF agency.[15] HHS data show that federal and state spending on work-related activities, such as subsidized employment, has declined in the last 3 years for which data are available (fiscal years 2011-2013) and has been under 8 percent of total TANF spending in each of these years.

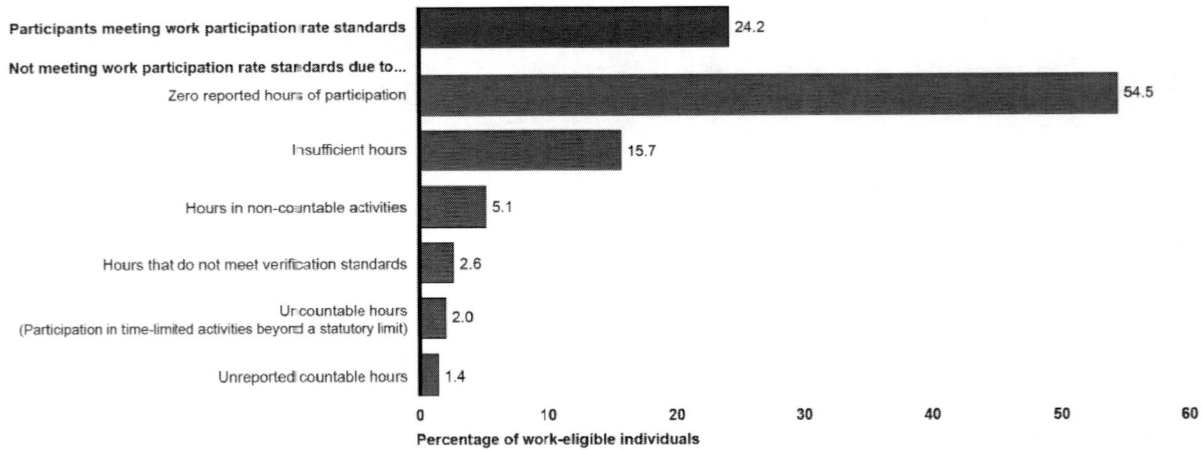

Source: GAO analysis of Department of Health and Human Services (HHS) data. | GAO-15-31.

Note: The number of individuals in each of the categories sum to more than 100 percent since a work-eligible individual could be included in more than one category. According to HHS, the percentage of work-eligible individuals that counts toward the work participation rate for the purpose of this analysis is likely to be lower than the official work participation rate for most states. This is due to methodological differences between the calculations. For example, work eligible individuals who are disregarded from the official work participation rate—such as certain single parent families with a child under the age of one or families subject to a work-related sanction—are included in this analysis.

Figure 1. Percentage of Work-Eligible Individuals by Participation Status, April 2011–June 2011.

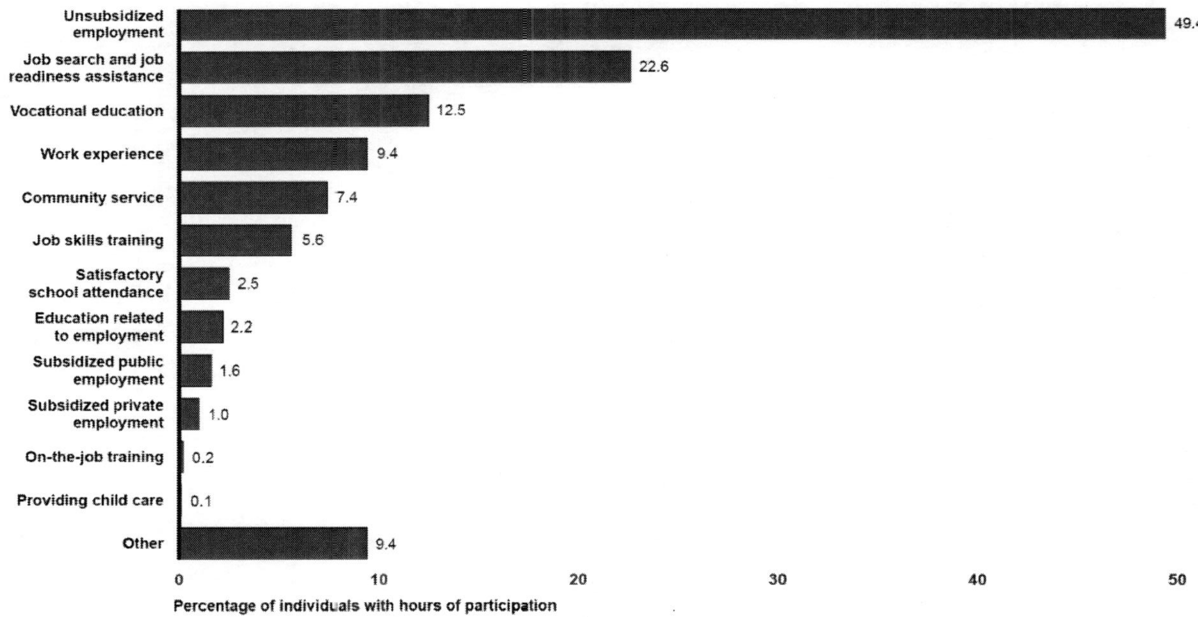

Source: GAO analysis of Department of Health and Human Services (HHS) data. | GAO-15-31.

Note: The number of individuals in each of the categories sum to more than 100 percent since a work-eligible individual could be included in more than one category.

Figure 2. Percentage of TANF Work-Eligible Individuals with Hours of Participation, by Work Activity, Fiscal Year 2011.

Almost half of individuals meeting the work participation rate standards did so through unsubsidized employment—working in a regular job while receiving cash assistance. This suggests that states' ability to meet the work participation rate relies heavily on the activities of individuals who are already able to work rather than providing special assistance to those who have the most difficulty finding and keeping jobs. In fiscal year 2011, unsubsidized employment was the most common work activity among individuals participating in at least one hour of a countable work activity per month.[16] Job search and job readiness assistance, followed by vocational education training, were the next most common activities (see fig. 2).

History of Welfare Program Experimentation, Research and State Waivers

Between 1987 and 1996, there was considerable experimentation with welfare-to-work programs under TANF's predecessor program, Aid to Families with Dependent Children (AFDC), as HHS granted waivers to states to test and evaluate new approaches. A body of HHS-sponsored research resulted, showing that welfare-to-work programs can increase employment and reduce welfare receipt. This research helped inform the creation of TANF. Between 1987 and 1996, 46 states received waivers from existing AFDC requirements to test and evaluate new approaches to improve employment outcomes for people on welfare. These initiatives were referred to as section 1115 waivers because they were granted under section 1115 of the Social Security Act.[17] According to HHS officials, HHS required states that applied for and received waivers from federal program requirements to have an independent organization evaluate its program change, supported by HHS and state funding.[18] These waiver initiatives included placing time limits on the receipt of benefits and strengthening work requirements, among others. According to HHS, many of the policies and concepts included in state waiver requests were later incorporated into TANF. States that received section 1115 waivers under AFDC were allowed, under PRWORA, to continue to operate under these waivers until their expiration. However, the last of these waivers expired in 2007, and no provision in law allowed these AFDC waivers to be extended. Questions have been raised as to whether HHS continues to have the authority under section 1115 to waive certain TANF program rules; this report does not address this issue.[19] Under law, HHS is required to conduct TANF and related research[20] and the agency supports a broad array of research and evaluations. See appendix III for a list of relevant recent and ongoing HHS-funded evaluations.

Evolution of the TANF Block Grant

Since the 1996 welfare law replaced AFDC with the TANF block grant and gave states flexibility to set spending priorities, they have used a smaller share of the grant to provide cash assistance.[21] Within the first 5 years of TANF, the number of families receiving cash assistance declined by over half and states shifted their TANF priorities to other forms of aid, or non-cash services. These can include any other services meeting TANF purposes, such as job preparation activities, child care and transportation assistance for parents, out-of-wedlock pregnancy prevention activities, and child welfare services. In fiscal year 1997, nationwide, states spent about 23 percent of federal TANF and state MOE funds on non-cash services. In contrast, states spent more than 66 percent of federal TANF and state MOE funds for these purposes in fiscal year 2013. While the TANF block grant still serves as the nation's major cash assistance program for low-income families with children, states have also increasingly used it as a flexible funding stream for supporting a broad range of allowable services. However, we previously reported that the accountability framework currently in place in federal law and regulations has not kept pace with this evolution. Our prior work found that TANF's accountability framework provides incomplete information on how states' non-cash services are contributing to TANF purposes. We noted that Congress may wish to consider ways to improve reporting and performance information so that it encompasses the full breadth of states' uses of TANF funds.[22] The composition of the overall TANF caseload has also changed, with the percentage of "child-only" cases increasing from about 23 percent in fiscal year 1998 to about 46 percent in fiscal year 2011. These cases consist of families receiving cash assistance on behalf of children only, in contrast to other cases in which adults in the families also receive benefits on their own behalf.[23] According to HHS, the increase in the percentage of child-only cases was primarily due to a sharp decline in the number of TANF cases with an eligible adult, rather than an increase in the number of child-only cases.

Hard-to-Employ TANF Recipients

Some TANF cash assistance recipients are work-ready while others face challenges that make them harder to employ. According to the preamble to a TANF final rule from 1999, several provisions of the law, including time limits, higher participation rate requirements, and fewer individual exemptions from participation requirements, taken together, suggest that states should serve more clients beyond just those who are job-ready.[24] However, some state TANF officials we interviewed for a 2012 report said the pressure to meet TANF work participation rate requirements causes them to focus on the "ready-to-work" cash assistance population, which can leave the "hard-to-employ" population without services. Health issues, disability, substance abuse, criminal records, domestic violence, limited education, and responsibilities for disabled children or parents can all constitute employment challenges for TANF recipients, who may need enhanced assistance to prepare for, find, and keep jobs. States may generally only count a family's participation in job readiness assistance, which can include mental health and substance abuse treatment, towards the work participation rate for up to 12 weeks in a year.

Selected State and Local Programs Reflect Elements of Four Promising Approaches

Research Indicates Several Promising Approaches for Increasing Employment and Earnings

A body of rigorous research points to four approaches that can be used to increase the employment and earnings of TANF cash assistance recipients: subsidized employment, treatment and employment services, career pathways, and modified work-first.[25] While still relevant, some of this research is based on programs that operated, at least in part, during TANF's predecessor program, AFDC, and have since ended; and some of these older studies focused on programs that predominantly targeted women. Some prior studies have also focused on individuals with education levels that are higher, on average, than the TANF population.

Further, although some of the programs discussed helped to increase participants' employment and earnings—and therefore, may have decreased dependence on public assistance—they did not necessarily increase household incomes. This is because the increased income from earnings can be offset by the loss of cash welfare, food assistance, and other support services. Ongoing research, including some of the current studies discussed below and in appendix III, aims to test updated versions of some of these approaches that might lead to longer-term results.

Research Snapshot: Subsidized Employment

Evaluation of Florida's Back to Work program

Florida's Back to Work program used American Recovery and Reinvestment Act of 2009 funding to create subsidized jobs. Administered by regional workforce boards, it operated in 2010 and placed about 5,600 individuals in subsidized jobs. For-profit, nonprofit, and public sector employers received subsidies that covered 80 to 95 percent of program participants' wages for 6 months. For-profit organizations were asked to commit to hiring the participants after the subsidy ended and non-profits were encouraged to do the same. Program participants experienced significantly greater increases in unsubsidized employment compared to individuals who were eligible but did not take part in subsidized employment. Participants experienced a nearly $4,000 average increase in earnings over their prior earnings compared to about a $1,500 average increase for the comparison group.

Source: Anne Roder and Mark Elliott, *Stimulating Opportunity: An Evaluation of ARRA-Funded Subsidized Employment Programs,* Economic Mobility Corporation, Inc. (New York, NY: September 2013).

- **Subsidized employment** – Subsidized employment broadly refers to the use of public funds to create or support temporary work opportunities for people who might otherwise be unemployed. One model of subsidized employment—transitional jobs—focuses on the hard-to-employ by providing temporary, wage-paying jobs, support services, and job placement help to individuals who have difficulty getting and holding jobs in the regular labor market. Subsidized employment programs have been used for decades to provide income support for people who are unable to find jobs in the regular labor market and improve employability for people with limited work experience.[26] These programs can vary, for example, in terms of the amount of wages that are subsidized; prospects for permanent, unsubsidized employment; the degree of worksite supervision provided; and whether the worker is employed directly or through an intermediary (see fig. 3).

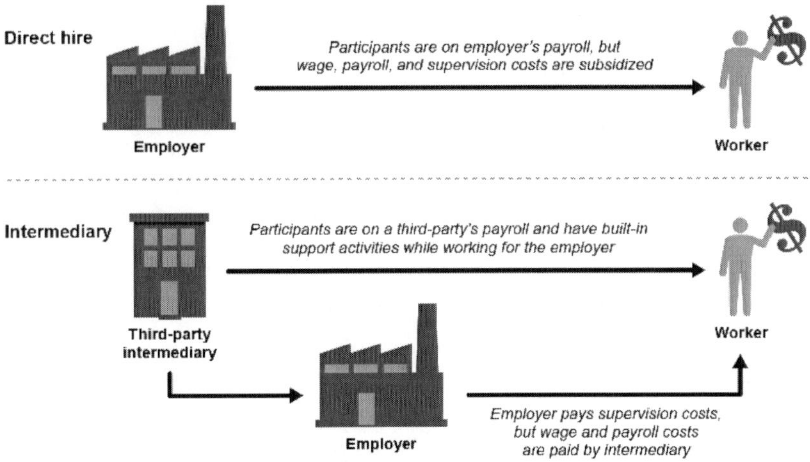

Source: GAO depiction of two subsidized employment program models, as described in Anne Roder and Mark Eliott, *Stimulating Opportunity: An Evaluation of ARRA-Funded Subsidized Employment Programs,* Economic Mobility Corporation, Inc. (New York, NY: September 2013). | GAO-15-31.

Figure 3. Two Subsidized Employment Models.

Research has shown that subsidized employment can increase employment and earnings, although some studies suggest that these gains may not last beyond the subsidized position. Nevertheless, these programs can provide individuals who are hard to employ with work experience and can have indirect effects, such as reduced recidivism among former prisoners. Subsidized employment programs in the 1970s and 1980s, during the time of TANF's predecessor program, yielded positive results on employment and earnings. One such demonstration project tested a model in which 10,000 welfare recipients in seven locations received 4 to 8 weeks of training and spent up to one year in subsidized positions as home health aides.[27] Most of the subsidized employment programs that produced long-term employment gains targeted women; disadvantaged men experienced fewer positive results following the period of subsidized employment.

Following welfare reform, transitional jobs gained traction as a strategy to increase the employability of TANF recipients. The theory behind this approach is that people best learn to work through working. Program staff can observe and coach participants on skills such as developing good work habits and dealing with coworkers to improve their future success in an unsubsidized job. Participants may be able to subsequently acquire jobs they would not otherwise have access to. Recent studies of transitional jobs programs have not shown sustained increases in employment, although these programs had indirect effects of reducing recidivism and reliance on welfare receipt.[28]

As part of the American Recovery and Reinvestment Act of 2009, Congress provided funding through the TANF Emergency Contingency Fund that in part helped states cover the costs of increased expenditures for subsidized employment programs.[29] Thirty-nine states and the District of Columbia reportedly used $1.3 billion from the Emergency Contingency Fund to create 260,000 subsidized jobs, according to research.[30] Although these efforts were not focused solely on TANF cash assistance recipients, experts we spoke with said the availability of additional funds renewed interest among states in subsidized employment. According to one study, these efforts involved the private sector in creating subsidized positions to a greater extent than in the past.[31]

Two coordinated research initiatives are currently under way to evaluate the "next generation" of subsidized employment programs. The HHS-funded Subsidized and Transitional Employment Demonstration is evaluating seven subsidized employment programs that target current, former, or potential TANF recipients, low-income noncustodial parents, and others. The Department of Labor-funded Enhanced Transitional Jobs Demonstration is evaluating seven sites for which it has provided grants for transitional jobs programs that target either non-custodial parents or former prisoners. HHS and the Department of Labor entered into a memorandum of agreement to coordinate these studies through shared data collection instruments and evaluation sites and coordinated reporting efforts. Both projects incorporate lessons from earlier research on transitional jobs and test whether providing subsidies to private employers can be effective for less job-ready participants. Reports on the results of these studies are scheduled for 2015 through 2018.

Research Snapshot: Treatment and Employment Services

Evaluation of New York City's Personal Roads to Individual Development and Employment (PRIDE)

New York City's PRIDE was a large-scale welfare-to-work program for recipients with work-limiting medical or mental health conditions. This program operated from 1999 to 2004, and served more than 30,000 people. Staff performed in-depth assessments of participants' work and education histories and medical conditions, then assigned them to activities—including unpaid work experience, education, and job placement assistance— that took account of their medical conditions. An evaluation of 3,000 randomly-assigned participants found that PRIDE significantly reduced the amount of welfare that participants received, in part because it generated increases in employment. Thirty-four percent of participants worked in jobs covered by unemployment insurance within 2 years after entering the study, compared to 27 percent of the control group. However, about two-thirds of participants never worked during the 2-year study period.

Source: Dan Bloom, Cynthia Miller, and Gilda Azurdia, Results from the Personal Roads to Individual Development and Employment (PRIDE) Program in New York City, a report prepared by MDRC at the request of the U.S. Department of Health and Human Services (July 2007).

- **Treatment and employment services** – This approach provides treatment for mental health needs, substance abuse, or a physical disability as well as employment services in different combinations and sequences (see fig. 4). The theory behind this approach is that treatment can help to stabilize a health condition to make steady work possible, while work experience can help participants learn how to manage problems that could otherwise prevent them from retaining a regular job.

Rigorous research has shown some limited impacts for this approach. Evaluation of one program that offered a mix of unpaid work experience, educational activities, and job search assistance to TANF recipients with work-limiting health conditions and disabilities showed, to some extent, increased employment that lasted for two years.[32] Another evaluation for a program in which staff visited participants' homes to teach them life skills showed substantial increases in employment and earnings for those considered very hard to employ, but the larger population of participants receiving services experienced only small increases in employment and earnings.[33]

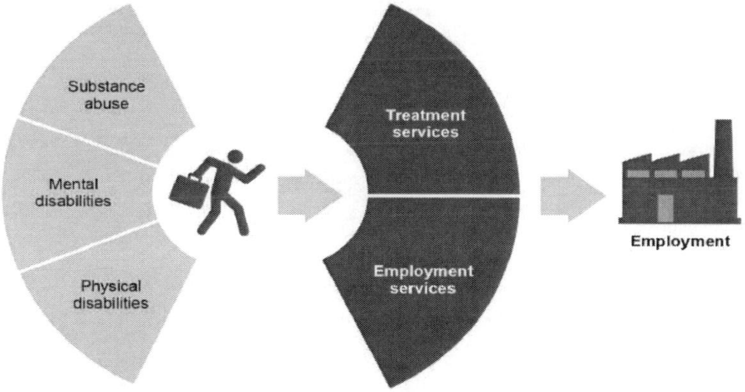

Source: GAO analysis. | GAO-15-31.

Figure 4. Treatment and Employment Services.

In terms of future research possibilities, HHS is considering whether emerging research from the fields of psychology and neuroscience on executive functioning—which is related to behaviors such as goal-setting, self-regulation, planning, and problem-solving—could help adults succeed in employment.[34] If so, it may have applications for TANF.

- **Career pathways** – This approach has been defined in different ways, but can involve providing contextual learning to prepare individuals of various skill levels to advance in a high-demand occupation or industry. Reading, writing, and math skills are taught using real-life materials and situations from the industry in which they will be used. Employers in the targeted sectors help to determine what skills are required for participants to become employed and advance their careers in growing industries. Workers of varying skill levels can use multiple entry or exit points to advance within a specific sector or occupational field and gain industry-recognized credentials through a clear sequence of education, training, or a combination of education and training. Participants are provided career counseling and other support services (see fig. 5).

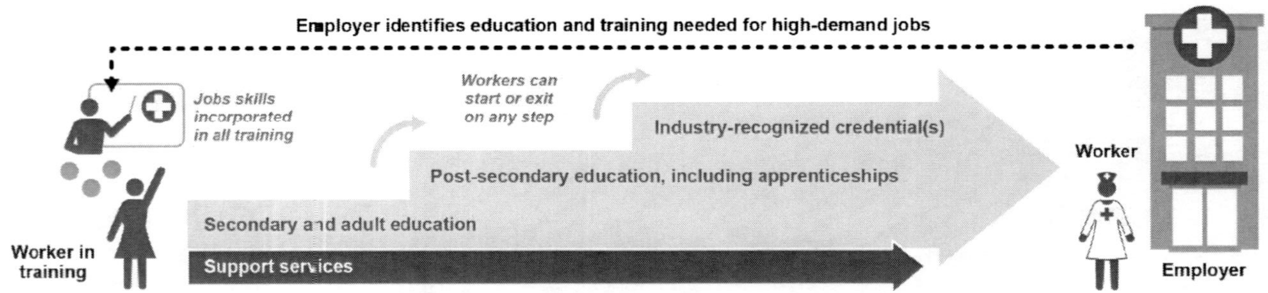

Source: GAO depiction of career pathways elements, as described in Social Policy Research Associates, *Career Pathways Toolkit. Six Key Elements for Success,* U.S. Department of Labor, (Washington, D.C. September 2011). | GAO-15-31.

Figure 5. Career Pathways.

This approach builds on results from a random-assignment evaluation of sector-based employment, indicating that programs offering sector-specific training can increase the employment and earnings of low-income individuals.[35] The approach is also informed by lessons from prior research showing that adult basic education alone has not been successful in connecting low-skilled individuals to jobs. Research on education-oriented welfare-to-work programs that operated in the 1980s and 1990s showed that the most successful programs offered short-term assignments that did not allow participants to "languish" in activities without making progress. This is in contrast to remedial education and GED preparation programs that either had difficulty retaining participants or kept them for years without clear progress. These prior findings informed a call for training that promotes career advancement, integrates basic education and skills training, and engages local employers, while providing support services to TANF recipients to improve program retention.[36]

As confirmed by HHS officials, there are no completed rigorous experimental impact studies of a comprehensive career pathways program, but HHS is funding relevant ongoing evaluations, as part of an inter-agency effort with the Departments of Education and Labor to promote the use of career pathways.[37]

One of the studies, known as the Innovative Strategies for Increasing Self-Sufficiency project, is a nine-site, random assignment evaluation of career pathway programs. Initiated in 2007, the study will last 10 years, and early results are expected in the next 2 to 3 years. HHS also has a research portfolio for evaluating health care-related education and training programs operated with Health Profession Opportunity Grants (HPOG). These grants are targeted to TANF recipients and other low-income individuals and aim to prepare them for occupations in the health care field that pay well and are expected to either experience labor shortages or be in high demand. Three of the HPOG grantees are to have site-specific impact evaluations as part of the Innovative Strategies for Increasing Self-Sufficiency project with reports expected in 2016.

An interim analysis of the impacts of HPOG is expected in June 2016. HHS expects that further follow-up analysis of both Innovative Strategies for Increasing Self-Sufficiency and HPOG impacts will be released in 2018.

Research Snapshot: Sector-Based Career Training

Public/Private Ventures' Sectoral Employment Impact Study

Results from Public/Private Ventures' Sectoral Employment Impact Study based on follow-up interviews 24 to 30 months after random assignment suggest that sectoral programs can increase the employment and earnings of traditionally disadvantaged workers. The study, launched in 2003, evaluated three sectoral programs that train workers for skilled positions in a range of industries, including healthcare, manufacturing, information technology, and construction. The study assessed impacts on employment, earnings, hourly wages and access to work-related benefits. Programs included in the study offered training that was focused on a specific sector or sectors and that took no more than a year to complete. Over the follow-up period, treatment group participants were employed an average of 1.3 months more than individuals in the control group. Individuals enrolled in training also earned about $4,500 more than individuals in the control group over a 2-year period and were also more likely to work in jobs with higher wages and benefits.

Sources: Sheila Maguire et al., Tuning In to Local Labor Markets: Findings from the Sectoral Employment Impact Study, Public/Private Ventures (Philadelphia, PA: 2010); and Alan Werner et al., Literature Review: Career Pathways Programs, OPRE Report #2013-24, Office of Planning, Research and Evaluation, Administration for Children and Families, Department of Health and Human Services (Washington, D.C.: June 24, 2013).

The Department of Education, Department of Labor, and HHS have jointly promoted the use of career pathways approaches as a promising strategy for helping adults acquire marketable skills and industry-recognized credentials.[38] The three agencies issued a Request for Information on the use of career pathways in April 2014 to inform policy development, strategic investments, and technical assistance activities and improve coordination of federal policy development.[39] The agencies have begun a joint analysis of responses to the Request for Information. According to HHS officials, this information will yield insights on (1) the benefits of and challenges to aligning diverse funding streams, programs, and stakeholders around career pathways systems; and (2) the current and potential future use of career pathways systems to help at-risk populations, including TANF cash assistance recipients, gain skills and access the middle class.

Research Snapshot: Modified Work-First Approach

The National Evaluation of Welfare-toWork Strategies (NEWWS)

NEWWS examined the long-term effects of 11 mandatory welfare-to-work programs, in seven sites, on welfare recipients and their children. These programs took different approaches to helping welfare recipients find jobs, advance in the labor market, and leave public assistance. During the 1990s, more than 40,000 single-parent families were tracked over 5-year follow-up periods. A Portland, Oregon program outperformed the other programs that were examined. It offered education or training to some participants, depending on the caseworkers' assessment of the individuals' skills and needs, and encouraged all participants to hold out for jobs that paid better than the minimum wage and offered stable employment. In the program's fifth year, it produced a 6.4 percent increase in employment and 14.6 percent increase in average earnings, compared to the control group.

Source: Gayle Hamilton, Moving People from Welfare to Work: Lessons from the National Evaluation of Welfare-toWork Strategies, Department of Health and Human Services, a report prepared by Manpower Demonstration Research Corporation at the request of the Department of Education (Washington, D.C.: 2002).

- **Modified work-first** – This approach entails a strong work focus and some upfront education or training, as needed (see fig 6). Research on welfare-to-work programs during the 1990s sought to test the effectiveness of programs that emphasized rapid employment ("work first") through mandatory job search compared to those that focused first on mandatory education and training. One program combined aspects of both of these approaches: it included a strong employment focus, the use of both job search and short-term education or training, and an emphasis on holding out for a good job, as opposed to participants taking the first job they were offered.[40]

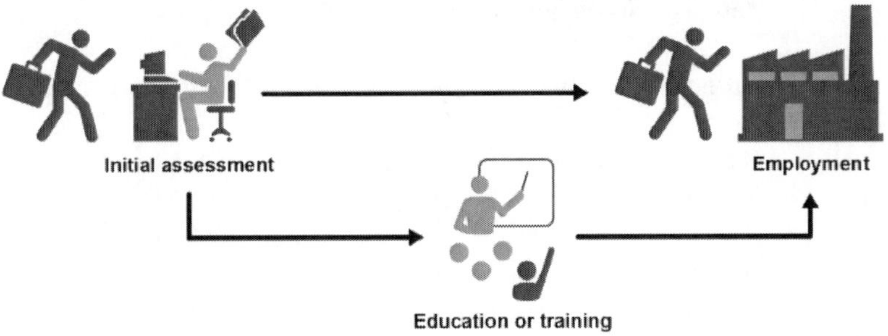

Source: GAO analysis. | GAO-15-31.

Figure 6. Modified Work-First Approach.

Research shows that programs using this approach increased employment and earnings and reduced welfare receipt. This approach appears more effective than programs that focus solely on education and training or solely on job search.

All Selected Programs Focus on Employment while Using Various Elements of the Approaches to Meet the Needs of Their Target Populations

We examined 10 ongoing programs that all help TANF cash assistance recipients to gain employment, using various different elements of the above cited promising approaches to meet a range of participant needs (see table 1).[41] These populations included those whose limited prior work experience prevented them from gaining employment on their own, those with one or more work-limiting characteristic such as a mental or physical disability or substance abuse problem, and those in need of additional skills to enter a new field or to increase their employability. All of the selected programs serve TANF recipients: 5 of the 10 serve TANF recipients exclusively, while the other programs serve a broader population.

Table 1. Characteristics of Selected Programs

	Program approach				Participant characteristics	
Program name	Subsidized employment	Treatment and employment services	Career pathways	Modified work first	Target population	Percentage ofparticipants whoreceive TANFcash assistance
San Francisco Jobs Now!	x				Adults divided into three tiers ranging from hard-to-employ to work-ready	41 %
Los Angeles County subsidized employment program	x				TANF recipients ranging from hard-to-employ to work-ready	100 %
Erie County (NY) Placing Individuals in Vital Opportunity Training (PIVOT)	x				Job-ready TANF recipients who had not found jobs on their own or during "job club" activities	100 %
Utah Licensed Clinical Therapists		x			TANF recipients with substance abuse, domestic violence, or mental health problems	100 %
New York City's Wellness, Comprehensive Assessment, Rehabilitation and Employment program (WeCARE)		x			Adults with mental or physical health or substance abuse problems	18 %

Table 1. (Continued)

	Program approach				Participant characteristics	
Program name	Subsidized employment	Treatment and employment services	Career pathways	Modified work first	Target population	Percentage ofparticipants whoreceive TANFcash assistance
Ramsey County (MN) Families Achieving Success Today (FAST)		x			Adults with mental or physical health or substance abuse problems	9 %
Washington State Integrated Basic Education and Skills Training (I-BEST)			x		Low-skilled and low-literacy adults	15 %
Minnesota Fast Training Resources and Credentialing Adult Career Pathways (FastTRAC)			x		Low-wage, low-skilled adults	18 %
Kentucky Ready to Work	x		x		TANF recipients interested in education; separate track for those with low literacy and math skills	100 %

	Program approach				Participant characteristics	
Program name	Subsidized employment	Treatment and employment services	Career pathways	Modified work first	Target population	Percentage ofparticipants whoreceive TANFcash assistance
District of Columbia TANF program				x	TANF recipients; separate tracks for those with different levels of education, experience, and skills and personal, health, or other barriers	100 %

Source: GAO analysis of information provided by experts and program officials. | GAO-15-31

Some of the programs we examined offered subsidized employment to those whose limited prior work experience prevents them from gaining employment on their own. For example:

- San Francisco's Jobs Now! program uses a community jobs model similar to a transitional employment program to place participants in employment positions. The program includes 6 months of subsidized employment and is targeted to those with limited experience or exposure to work. Some participants are placed in public service training programs where they are employed with the local human services agency or other city departments like the Office of Parks and Recreation. Other participants who are more job ready are placed in a wage-subsidy program with private businesses. Under this program tier, Jobs Now! subsidizes 100 percent of the wage for the first month, 75 percent for the second month, and $1,000 for the next 3 months. Employers also agree to make a good faith effort to retain the employee after the subsidy ends. Administrators reported that the retention rate with private employers—once the subsidy ends—is between 75 and 80 percent.
- Similarly, Erie County, New York's PIVOT wage subsidy program requires a commitment from employers to hire participants after the wage subsidy ends. PIVOT is designed to serve those TANF recipients who are among the more work-ready, but who did not find jobs on their own during previous job search activities. When participants are referred to the program through the local TANF agency, they receive a skills assessment and enter a job-readiness training program for 45 days while their eligibility is being determined. Participants are screened to match their skill levels with employer needs. PIVOT places participants in local employment—in industries such as banking, hospitality, legal services, manufacturing, health, and childcare—for 6 months during job training. Participants' days are typically split between a work experience program and other work activities such as GED classes or barrier remediation, such as English lessons for refugees with language barriers.
- Los Angeles County's large subsidized employment program includes a component in which participants can gain work experience with for-profits, nonprofits or government agencies, and an on-the-job training component that places participants with private sector employers. For the latter, a subsidy for the participants' wages is sent to a private job

provider during the first two months of employment. After those 60 days, the wage is paid directly by the employer, who receives $350 for each part-time employee and $500 for each full-time employee.

Three of the ten programs we examined used the treatment and employment services approach to serve participants with one or more physical or mental disabilities, substance abuse, or other work-limiting characteristics.

- Utah's Licensed Clinical Therapist program provides services for clients with substance abuse, domestic violence, and mental health problems. An administrator said participants often enter the program under emotional turmoil that—if untreated—would prevent them from gaining stable employment. To address this need, clients receive a clinical assessment to diagnose mental health problems and they can participate in clinical therapy sessions offered by the program in combination with job search and resume building activities.
- New York City WeCARE was designed to provide comprehensive services to hard-to-employ clients with mental or physical health needs or substance abuse problems. The program uses an in-house comprehensive assessment of physical, psychological, and social needs by a board-certified doctor and social worker to determine whether a client is fully employable, can participate in work-related activities with limitations, needs treatment to stabilize a condition before engaging in work-related activities, or if the client could be eligible for federal disability benefits. One important program element is flexibility. For example, participants have a window of several days to make a scheduled appointment. A contractor told us that by offering flexibility, the program is better able to engage participants whom other programs might automatically sanction for non-participation.[42]
- Ramsey County, Minnesota's FAST program is a partnership between agencies that co-locate services like mental health treatment, vocational rehabilitation, community health care, and TANF employment supports. Administrators said with the right supports and an individualized service plan, clients with mental or physical health or substance abuse problems –who are not eligible for federal disability benefits—can gain employment. FAST contracts services with Goodwill/Easter Seals, which provides day-to-day supervision of participants and facilitates the individual placement and supports

created for them. Home visits are used as needed to assess families' needs, and family supports, including employment retention services, can last up to 9 months or longer.

Three of the ten programs we examined used multiple elements of the sector-based career pathways approach to increase the skills of participants looking to enter a new field or increase their employability.

- Washington State's I-BEST program was developed to help participants increase their literacy and basic skills while earning certificates or degrees in order to qualify for in-demand jobs. The program is offered in 34 community and technical colleges in the state. The program curriculum is based on regional job market demands and resources. A college must demonstrate local demand for a career program and show that those who complete the program will be able to exit it and receive an average wage of $13/hour or more. Program administrators said they believe their program is successful because of its team-taught, integrated service delivery model. Within I-BEST classrooms, two instructors work together to bolster basic skills while integrating career-related content into students' curriculum. Since the program's founding about 10 years ago, more than 200 career programs in fields such as health care, early childhood education, and advanced manufacturing have been approved by the Washington State Board for Community and Technical Colleges.
- The Minnesota FastTRAC program aims to move low-wage, low-skilled adults into credit-bearing training. Participants typically enter the program after being referred by various sources including local TANF and workforce programs. Participants are screened to determine their education level and needs. Similar to the I-BEST program, clients then go to classroom-based programs, in which instruction in math and reading is provided within the context of a profession like healthcare. Clients may also participate in some job shadowing during this period.
- Similarly, Kentucky officials perceived a need to increase educational attainment among the TANF population to improve their employability and launched the Ready to Work program about 16 years ago. The program is run statewide through the Kentucky Community and Technical College System. Unlike the I-BEST program, which focuses specifically on high-demand occupations,

Ready to Work allows participants to select classes from the full catalogue of local courses.

However, the program does offer counseling on job prospects in various career tracks. Participants also engage in on- or off-campus work study positions with public and private employers that are subsidized using TANF funds and connected to each participant's program of study and career goal.

All of the programs we examined used some form of assessment to identify participants' service needs. Across the programs, factors assessed included skill levels, work history, interests, and physical and mental health. Additionally six of the 10 programs structured services or program offerings in two or more tiers or employment tracks for the purpose of better targeting the needs of participants.

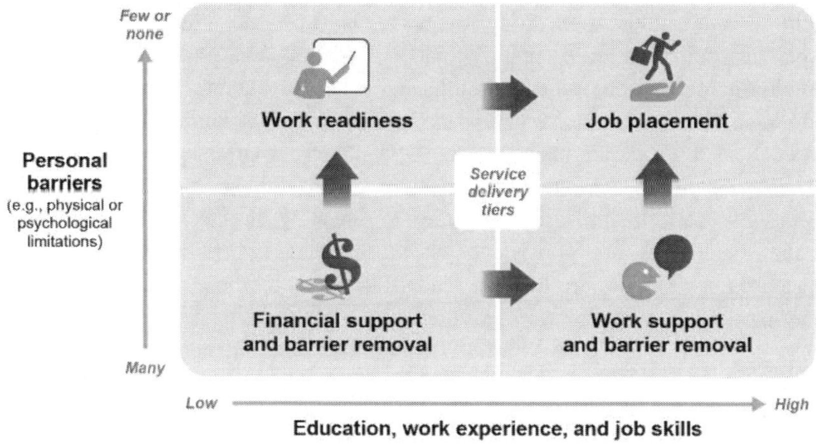

Source: GAO presentation of D.C. Temporary Assistance for Needy Families (TANF) program's service delivery model. | GAO-15-31.

Figure 7. D.C. TANF Program's Service Delivery Model.

- For example, the D.C. TANF program, which uses elements of a modified work-first approach, was redesigned in 2008-2009 in response to complaints that under the program's "one size fits all" service delivery model, job-ready clients and those with significant barriers to employment were receiving the same services. Under the redesign, a continuum of services is available based on the client's needs at assessment. Clients are categorized into a service delivery tier based on their education, experience, and skills, as well as barriers they may face (see fig 7).

Selected Programs Emphasize Work Participation Rate to Varying Degrees

Although the programs we examined were all focused on work, they varied in the extent to which they were structured to help their states meet TANF's work participation rate requirements, according to state and program officials. Contributing to the work participation rate, such as by requiring participants to meet specific federally-defined hours and activities requirements, was a goal of 5 of the 10 programs, for at least some portion of the participants served. For example, a Kentucky Ready to Work program administrator said its work study component is its biggest asset for meeting the work participation rate requirements. Students are placed in private-employment positions when possible and when positions are not available, administrators said students can work on campus or in volunteer positions to meet their hours requirements. In the D.C. TANF program, participants have different requirements depending on their service delivery tier. For example, job-ready participants are expected to meet both hours and activity requirements that are consistent with the federal work participation rate standards. Those who are less job ready must meet the hour requirements but may participate in any mix of activities even if it they do not count toward the District's work participation rate. An administrator told us the D.C. TANF program was designed based on what they thought would work best to get participants employed and with the expectation that this will also result in meeting the work participation rate requirements.

The work participation rate requirement was given less emphasis by the other five programs we examined, according to state and program officials. These administrators said their programs did not emphasize the work participation rate because of a conscious choice to prioritize other program goals, or because their programs served too few work-eligible TANF recipients to affect the state's rate. Nearly all (9 of the 10 programs we examined) were components of larger TANF programs, meaning that states and localities may have a variety of other mechanisms for meeting the work participation rate requirements beyond these programs. Even without a strong emphasis on the work participation rate, these programs—like those that did emphasize the work participation rate—still maintained an employment focus and some offered activities that at least partially counted toward the work participation rate.

Administrators in Los Angeles County's subsidized employment program said they do not over-emphasize contributing toward the work participation rate requirements, but instead focus on placing participants in work. Similar to the D.C. TANF program—where addressing participants' barriers and progressively increasing their engagement over time is thought to contribute to the work participation rate and increase long-term stable employment—Los Angeles County officials said if participants can be placed in employment, meeting the requirement is typically not an issue. Additionally, administrators said that because California allows clients to participate in some activities for longer durations than can be counted toward the federal requirement, they focus on keeping people engaged in work-related activities under the state rules.[43]

Because TANF cash assistance beneficiaries comprise only 15 percent of Washington State's I-BEST participants, contributing toward the work participation rate is not an explicit goal of this career pathways program. However, administrators said that time spent in the program's short-term training can count toward meeting the work participation rate requirements. Some experts who were knowledgeable about career pathways programs nationwide told us that some states have a misperception that the career pathways approach is not allowable under TANF rules, since only 12 months of vocational education training can be counted toward the work participation rate. However, HHS officials told us that states can allow TANF recipients to combine education with other work activities that count toward the work participation rate, meaning that within certain constraints, activities under the career pathways approach can be counted toward the work participation rate requirements. Some experts said that formal guidance from HHS, among other agencies, clarifying this fact might encourage broader use. Internal control standards for the federal government state that information should be communicated to managers and others who need it in a form that enables them to carry out their responsibilities.[44] In TANF's decentralized block grant environment, state and local officials make many program decisions and it is important that they also receive pertinent information in a form that enables them to carry out their duties and responsibilities efficiently and effectively. While HHS's Administration for Children and Families has conducted webinars and regional workshops to help guide TANF agencies in the implementation of career pathways approaches, the agency has not issued any such formal guidance. Greater clarity regarding how activities related to the career pathways approach may be allowable under TANF rules could address misperceptions and encourage more widespread use of this approach by state and local TANF agencies.

EXPERTISE AND DEDICATED FUNDS FACILITATED THE USE OF PROMISING APPROACHES, BUT THE TANF PROGRAM LACKS INCENTIVES FOR WIDER ADOPTION OR TESTING

The Selected Programs Benefitted from Partner Expertise and Dedicated Funding

Nearly all of the 10 programs we examined that currently use elements of promising approaches drew on expertise beyond the state or local TANF agency (see table 2). Nine of these programs involved partnerships with organizations and agencies such as community college systems, workforce agencies, and nonprofit organizations or contracted vendors. These partnerships provided the selected programs with access to the experience and expertise of a range of partners. For example:

- Officials with the Los Angeles County TANF agency noted that partnership with a local workforce agency is a key facilitating factor in its subsidized employment program. The workforce agency has acted as the employer of record for payroll and insurance purposes, and had existing employer relationships, so the TANF agency did not need to develop these capacities.
- While Kentucky's Ready to Work program is entirely funded by TANF, the program is administered by the state's community college system, and its case managers are located on campus and familiar with the college environment. According to program officials, clients generally pay their tuition through federal Pell Grants, so Ready to Work case managers help clients complete financial aid applications and ensure they remain eligible for the grants.
- Officials with Ramsey County, Minnesota's FAST program that seeks to engage individuals with disabilities in work reported that the experience and credibility of the initiative's lead nonprofit partner was

a key facilitating factor. They particularly valued the nonprofit's previous experience working with both rehabilitation and employment services, as opposed to other contractors that have only operated in the TANF employment context.

Table 2. Selected Program Partner Organizations and Technical Assistance

	Partner organizations in addition to state or local TANF agency			
Program name	Community college system	Workforce agency	Nonprofit or vendor	Received technical assistance
San Francisco Jobs Now!			•	
Los Angeles County subsidized employment program		•		•
Erie County (NY) Placing Individuals in Vital Opportunity Training (PIVOT)			•	•
Utah Licensed Clinical Therapists		a		
New York City's Wellness, Comprehensive Assessment, Rehabilitation and Employment program (WeCARE)			•	
Ramsey County (MN) Families Achieving Success Today (FAST)		•	•	•
Washington State Integrated Basic Education and Skills Training (I-BEST)	•			
Minnesota Fast Training Resources and Credentialing Adult Career Pathways (FastTRAC)	•	•	•	•
Kentucky Ready to Work	•			•
District of Columbia TANF program			•	•

Source: GAO summary of information provided by program officials. | GAO-15-31
[a]Utah's TANF program is administered by the state workforce agency.

Six of the programs also received technical assistance from a federal agency or nonprofit, such as a policy research organization or foundation. For example, Minnesota officials cited participation in the federal Career Pathways Institute as an important step in the development of the state's career pathways program.[45]

Officials said participation in technical assistance activities connected them with many other programs that influenced elements of their work. Officials in Los Angeles and Ramsey County, Minnesota, said that taking part in an evaluation conducted by a research organization helped inform their program models, and Ramsey County officials said their participation had enabled them to access additional resources, such as training from national experts.

Decisions by state and local policymakers to dedicate funds for the selected programs also facilitated the use of promising approaches, according to program officials.

We have previously reported that when federal TANF funds are allocated to states, states do not necessarily direct the funding to state welfare agencies, but may allocate funds to support various programs depending on legislative priorities (see fig. 8). Officials with 7 of the 10 programs we interviewed noted that state or local funding decisions had facilitated their use of promising approaches.[46] For example, officials with the District of Columbia TANF program noted that the allocation of additional funding has been the key factor that has allowed the agency to continue to support its modified work-first approach.

Officials reported that the approach requires more staff resources to assess clients' work readiness and determine appropriate activities than does the agency's prior model of "one size fits all." The allocation of additional resources has allowed the agency to support these staff.

The allocation of additional funds by state and local governments also facilitated San Francisco's use of a subsidized employment approach for TANF cash assistance recipients, according to program officials. They reported that these funds have supported the agency's ability to increase its wage subsidy in an effort to attract higher-wage employers.

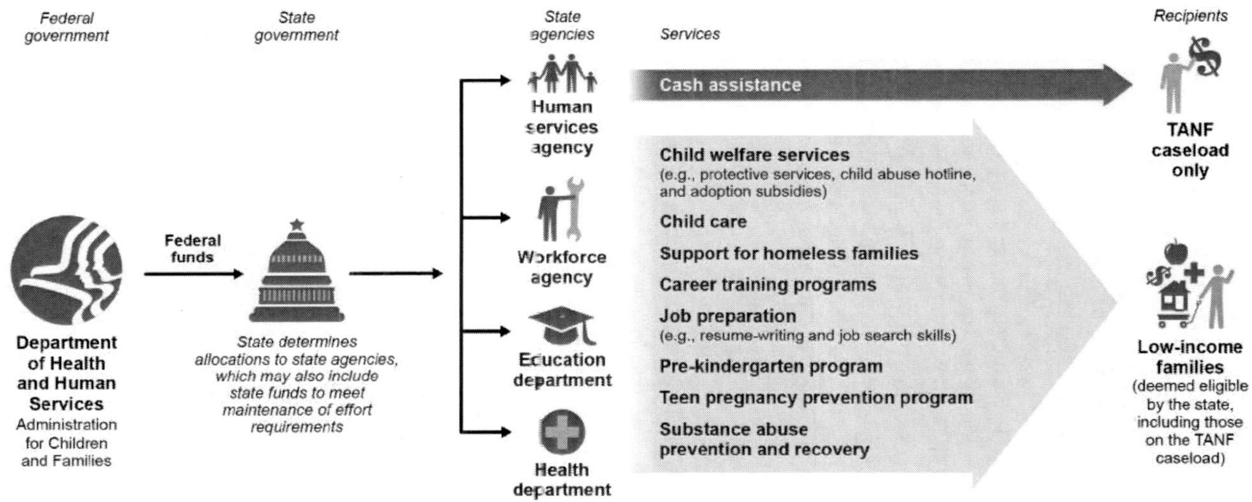

Source: GAO analysis based on examples of programs and services funded by Temporary Assistance for Needy Families (TANF) in various states. | GAO-15-31.

Figure 8. Example of Possible Allocation of TANF Funds by a State.

Additionally, in 3 of the 10 programs, TANF funds and other funding sources were mixed to support the program, which served both TANF clients and other low-income populations. For example, New York City's WeCARE program combined TANF funds with state and local funds to serve 24,000 daily participants, which included TANF cash assistance recipients as well as low-income single adults and childless couples with clinical barriers to employment who received cash assistance through a state-funded program. These funding sources were combined to award contracts to vendors that provide treatment and employment services to any client regardless of his or her program affiliation. Officials with Minnesota's FastTRAC career pathways program said that initial funding for their program came from a foundation grant and subsequently from funds available under the American Recovery and Reinvestment Act of 2009. They noted that the state has been able to maintain the program after that funding was no longer available because the program is a partnership with multiple state agencies and a nonprofit organization, most of whom contribute some funding. These funds are combined and then sent to local providers of career pathways programs through competitive grants. While Minnesota officials suggested that combining resources across partners was key to their program, they also noted the challenges of reconciling different funding streams and performance measures. Experts knowledgeable about career pathways programs nationwide echoed these concerns to us. They suggested a need for federal guidance to clarify how various sources of federal funds can be used to support these programs, and that some TANF programs may be reluctant to use a career pathways approach in the absence of a clear statement that use of TANF funds for career pathways programs is explicitly allowable. As noted above, HHS has provided some information related to career pathways, but has not issued formal guidance. Consistent with internal control standards, guidance could help state and local officials to better carry out their responsibilities. Without explicit clarification that TANF funds may be used to finance career pathways activities, some state and local TANF agencies may be discouraged from attempting this approach.

TANF Lacks Incentives for the Broader Adoption and Testing of Promising Approaches

As structured, the TANF program lacks incentives to encourage broader adoption of promising approaches by large numbers of state and local TANF agencies. The federal law that created TANF established a goal of increasing job preparation and employment, and included a provision addressing the development and evaluation of innovative approaches for reducing welfare dependency.[47] However, several TANF program characteristics may not encourage states to adopt and test new approaches for increasing the employment and earnings of cash assistance recipients. HHS's authority over many aspects of TANF is limited and it has not proposed legislative changes to address these areas. Without federal action, adoption and evaluation of promising approaches may continue to be limited to select states and localities, leaving TANF recipients in other locations without access to these promising approaches.

Program Design and Funding

TANF leaves many program design and funding choices to states. The law that created the TANF block grant established a goal of state flexibility, and restricted HHS's regulatory authority over the states except to the extent expressly provided in the law. 48 This flexibility allows for multi-agency partnerships that can facilitate the use of promising approaches, as discussed above. It also allows states to spend TANF funds on a wide range of programs and services that are not necessarily related to welfare-to-work activities, as long as these services support one of TANF's four statutory purposes.[49] In a 2012 report, we found that states spent significant amounts of TANF funds on services such as child welfare or child care, and that state use of federal TANF funds for these and other services can create tensions and trade-offs in state funding decisions.[50] As a result, any additional resources needed for implementing more costly promising approaches for TANF cash assistance clients may compete with other allowable uses of TANF funds. Officials with three programs we interviewed that exclusively use TANF funds to implement elements of promising approaches noted that their programs had been continuously funded for many years and suggested that it would be difficult to find funding for the programs were they beginning today.

Work Participation Rate Requirements

Additionally, the federal work participation rate requirements do not necessarily work as an incentive for states to implement certain promising approaches, according to our interviews and prior work. Some experts and HHS officials we interviewed suggested that limits on the amount of time that certain job readiness and training activities may be counted toward a state's work participation rate 51 may discourage states from pursuing approaches that involve longer-term treatment or education. We have previously reported the concerns of state and local TANF officials that these limits do not allow sufficient time to address barriers to work for clients who have been out of the workforce for an extended period of time or to train clients for higher-wage employment that will prevent them from needing assistance in the future.

Officials with 5 of the 10 programs we interviewed that were using promising approaches also expressed concerns about the limits. For example, officials with Ramsey County Minnesota's treatment and employment services program said the TANF work activities rules do not provide enough flexibility for families coping with mental illness in that the time limit on job search and job readiness assistance and the 20-hour minimum for core work activities are not realistic for all.[52] As a result, officials said most clients in the program receive cash assistance through a state program rather than through TANF.[53] Yet, serving such clients through a state program instead of TANF likely limits the program's replicabilty in other state or local TANF agencies, as not all states may be willing to devote state funds for this purpose.[54] Officials with Kentucky's Ready to Work program reported that the 12-month limit on counting vocational educational training toward the work participation rate[55] has caused the program to rely more heavily on its work-study subsidized employment component, which has increased the program's cost. Further, one official said that while the subsidized work-study component is a critical program feature, the expectation that clients will work at least 20 hours a week once they have exhausted their allowable full-time education may affect academic outcomes.

The work activity limits only apply to what states may count toward the work participation rate and do not prevent states from allowing clients to engage in these activities for longer periods of time. However, several experts we interviewed explained that many state policies on activities that are available to clients are shaped by the work participation rate requirements. That is, some states may design their programs to provide and support only those activities that count toward the work participation rate, while other states also provide and support activities that do not count toward the rate. In addition, we have previously found that states have relied on a combination of factors allowed in law to reduce the percentage of families they needed to engage in work to meet their work participation rate requirements.[56] According to the most recent data available from fiscal year 2011, 23 states used these factors to reduce their required work participation rate for all TANF families from 50 percent to 0 percent. As a result, states may have less incentive to use promising approaches to engage hard-to-employ individuals in work activities, as they can meet their work participation rate requirements without engaging these individuals. In 2013, we noted that the work participation rate is complex and that any potential changes to the measure would likely have a profound impact on state TANF programs.[57]

Research and Evaluation

Finally, interviews conducted for this report and our previous work indicate that state and local TANF agencies have little incentive to test the effectiveness of new approaches. While several program administrators cited short-term or anecdotal evidence that their programs may contribute to increases in employment and earnings, only 4 of the 10 programs had undergone or were currently involved in a rigorous impact evaluation.[58]

States are not required to conduct impact evaluations of their TANF programs under federal TANF law, although these evaluations can provide useful information on program effectiveness. A rigorous evaluation impact study with a random assignment design allows for comparison with a control group in order to distinguish the program's influence from other factors.

Officials with some of the programs that had not undergone rigorous evaluations said they had not participated in these studies because of concerns about administrative burden, the newness of the program, or that a portion of their caseload would not receive services or count toward the work participation rate. Local Minnesota FastTRAC contractors said long-term follow ups with clients who had left the program would be burdensome to staff, who need to focus on newer or existing participants' needs. An official with the D.C. TANF program said it had not yet been evaluated formally because the program had only recently been redesigned. A Kentucky Ready to Work administrator said the program has not been rigorously evaluated through a random assignment study. The administrator said this was because the state TANF agency does not want to deny services to anyone who is eligible as a result of being assigned to a control group or miss an opportunity to contribute toward the work participation rate.[59] An administrator at one site that was undergoing a rigorous impact evaluation said that because only half of study participants would be selected for the program, recruitment for the study was challenging.

We have previously found that although HHS has a strong tradition of leading and supporting rigorous welfare research, there are fewer incentives for states to evaluate their programs under TANF than existed under the previous welfare program with its evaluation and funding provisions.[60] Indeed, although HHS maintains an active research agenda, TANF agency participation in some recent and ongoing HHS evaluations has been limited. For example, none of the four sites in the recently-completed Enhanced Services for the Hard-to-Employ Demonstration and Evaluation were TANF agencies.[61] In addition, in two ongoing evaluations of career pathways programs, participating sites consist primarily of community colleges and workforce agencies. According to HHS, these sites vary in the extent to which they serve TANF cash assistance recipients.[62] An HHS official we interviewed reported that engaging TANF programs in evaluations of promising approaches is difficult because of the administrative burden on the state or locality. Officials added that HHS has no authority to require state agency participation in research and evaluation and no dedicated funding to provide states or localities incentives to participate. However, HHS officials also noted that often entities beyond TANF agencies serve TANF cash assistance recipients and research findings are still relevant for these partners. HHS has also taken steps to share research findings with local TANF programs, welfare researchers, and policymakers. For example, the agency has sponsored an annual Welfare Research and Evaluation Conference to share evaluations of welfare reform and formulate ways to incorporate these findings in the design and implementation of programs since 1998. HHS also makes research results available through presentations at other conferences related to welfare and low-income issues, their agency websites, and online announcements sent to subscribers.

CONCLUSION

While the 10 state and local programs we examined are making use of some promising approaches for moving TANF recipients into employment and increasing their earnings, incentives are lacking for large numbers of state and local TANF agencies to adopt and test such approaches under the structure of the TANF program. This suggests a loss of opportunity. Data already suggest that state TANF programs currently engage recipients in a relatively limited range of activities and that more TANF recipients could be engaged in activities that are work-related. TANF's goals include ending needy families' dependence on government benefits by promoting work. However, the program's block grant structure means that many policy decisions are decentralized, and HHS has limited authority in directing state programmatic choices. This tends to leave innovation to individual localities and states. Yet other allowable uses of TANF funds compete with the adoption of promising welfare-to-work approaches. Further, limited participation by TANF agencies in HHS evaluations may slow the development and adoption of new promising approaches, leaving TANF without a continuous improvement process. In announcing its intention to exercise waiver authority, HHS noted that the purpose of its proposed waivers was to test alternative and innovative strategies, policies, and procedures designed to improve employment outcomes for needy families. However, as HHS officials told us, no state has applied for a waiver since its announcement in 2012. While we are not taking a position on whether HHS has authority to issue waivers, it is clear that this strategy has not encouraged states to innovate and test new approaches. We recognize that PRWORA limits HHS's authority over state program and funding choices and evaluations of state programs. Yet, HHS, as the federal agency that oversees TANF, is positioned to identify, suggest, and work in consultation with Congress on potential changes that would address the lack of incentives for states to adopt promising approaches. Absent federal action, adoption and evaluation of promising approaches may continue to be limited to select states and localities, leaving TANF recipients in other locations without access to these promising approaches. In the meantime, at least one promising approach—career pathways—appears to suffer from misperceptions about whether activities under the career pathways approach can be counted toward the work participation rate, or whether the career pathways approach is allowable with TANF funds. Without clarification that it is, indeed, allowable, TANF agencies may be discouraged from attempting it.

Recommendations for Executive Action

To encourage broader adoption and evaluation of promising approaches and address impediments to the use of the career pathways approach among TANF agencies, we recommend that HHS should take the following two actions:

- In consultation with Congress, identify potential changes that would address the lack of incentives for states and localities to adopt promising approaches and then develop and submit a legislative proposal outlining those changes.
- Issue formal guidance to clarify how activities under the career pathways approach can be countable for the purpose of the work

participation rate and that TANF funds may be used to finance the career pathways approach.

AGENCY COMMENTS AND OUR EVALUATION

We provided a draft of this report to HHS, the Department of Education, and the Department of Labor. The Departments of Education and Labor did not have comments. HHS provided written comments, in which the agency generally concurred with our recommendations. HHS also provided technical comments that we incorporated, as appropriate.

HHS agreed with our recommendation that the agency consult with Congress on ways to address the lack of incentives for states and localities to adopt promising employment-focused approaches. HHS noted that in the Administration's Fiscal Year 2015 Budget Request, it stated, "when Congress takes up reauthorization, the Administration will be prepared to work with lawmakers to strengthen the program's effectiveness in accomplishing its goals. This effort should include using performance indicators to drive program improvement and ensuring that states have the flexibility to engage recipients in the most effective activities to promote success in the workforce, including families with serious barriers to employment." The budget request also included a legislative proposal to increase incentives for states to implement or strengthen subsidized employment programs by creating a new initiative funded by diverting existing TANF Contingency Funds to this new use. We were aware of these points in HHS's budget request and maintain that HHS should develop more concrete proposals to address the lack of incentives within the TANF program itself, and note that the agency need not wait for Congress to take up reauthorization to do so. HHS also noted that it has sponsored a large body of research that helps federal policy makers understand the wide variety of services provided by state TANF programs and provides credible information to state TANF decision-makers about possible innovative and effective approaches to serving their clients. At the same time, the agency acknowledged that gaps remain in the research on effective employment-focused approaches for low-income families and noted that additional research is needed.

HHS also agreed with our recommendation that the agency issue formal guidance to clarify how the career pathways approach can be used by TANF agencies. HHS said that it will issue a formal Information Memorandum on the implementation of career pathways approaches in TANF, as part of the agency's ongoing technical assistance efforts. It also elaborated on the various ways it has promoted career pathways and other employment-focused approaches in recent years, as we acknowledged in the report. In addition to the need for guidance, HHS said that the 12-month limit on counting vocational education training toward the work participation rate is a constraint to the implementation of career pathways models in TANF programs. However, as we note in our report, states may allow TANF recipients to combine education with other work activities that count toward the work participation rate. Better clarification of this fact through formal guidance should help to address state misperceptions that the time limit on counting vocational education training prohibits the use of career pathways approaches.

Kay E. Brown,
Director
Education, Workforce, and Income Security Issues

APPENDIX I: OBJECTIVES, SCOPE, AND METHODOLOGY

Our report (1) reviews some approaches that have been identified as holding promise to engage TANF recipients in employment and increase their earnings and examines ways in which selected states and localities have used them, and (2) identifies factors that influence the use of these and other promising approaches.

To first identify promising approaches, we reviewed research summaries and syntheses of rigorous research on approaches for engaging TANF recipients in employment and increasing their earnings.[1] We primarily focused on studies that used a random assignment (experimental) research design. This type of design compares the outcomes for groups that were randomly assigned either to the treatment or to a nonparticipating control group before the intervention, in an effort to control for any systematic difference between the groups that could account for a difference in their outcomes. A difference in these groups' outcomes is believed to represent the program's impact.[2] To help compile the research we reviewed, we conducted a literature search of 12 research databases, including EconLit, ProQuest Research Library, and Social Services Abstracts, using search terms such as "welfare to work." Our intent was not to describe all possible promising approaches, but rather to identify some key approaches.

We considered approaches to be “promising” if a rigorous evaluation had determined that a program using this approach contributed to increased employment, income, or earnings, or reduced welfare receipt. Not all programs using the approach had to yield positive results in order for the approach to be considered promising. We realize that there is variation in how these approaches are implemented. Although a comprehensive career pathways program has not yet been rigorously evaluated, we included this approach because it was based on a rigorous evaluation of sector-based career training and lessons from other prior rigorous evaluations.

We sought input on our list of approaches from researchers with MDRC, a nonprofit, nonpartisan education and social policy research organization. We also validated our list of approaches through the process of seeking expert nominations for programs currently using these approaches. For example, based on our review of the literature, we initially identified earnings supplements—the practice of supplementing low-wage workers’ earnings with incentives to encourage employment and employment retention—as a possible promising approach. However, because we did not find any current examples of this approach being used to serve TANF cash assistance recipients, we did not include it in our final list of promising approaches.

To identify state and local programs that are currently using these approaches to serve TANF cash assistance recipients, we interviewed cognizant researchers; officials from the Department of Health and Human Services (HHS), the Department of Labor, and the Department of Education; and others with TANF expertise. We selected 12 experts based on their knowledge of the research and efforts under way at the state and local level, as well as to reflect a range of perspectives on welfare-to-work issues. We identified them through our literature review and through referrals from other experts. We asked the experts and agency officials to identify state and local programs that are currently using the promising approaches we identified through our literature review to serve TANF cash assistance recipients. We asked the experts to indicate the specific reasons why they recommended these programs and whether evaluation results or outcome data were available for the programs; however, these programs have generally not been rigorously evaluated.

From the programs identified by experts, we selected 10 programs to profile (located in 6 states—California, Kentucky, Minnesota, New York, Utah, and Washington—and the District of Columbia) to reflect diversity in approaches used, economic conditions, demographics, and geographic regions. We also considered how the program was connected to TANF and whether the program was in an area where TANF is state- or countyadministered.[3] We did not report on work participation rates for the states in which these programs are operated because some are state programs and others are locally administered. Work participation rates are calculated only on the state level by HHS, based on data reported by the states, and generally available after the end of the fiscal year. We conducted in-depth interviews, by phone and through four site visits, with program administrators and state and local TANF officials to learn about key program features that help increase employment and earnings. For 3 programs, we also interviewed local contractors. We obtained views from experts; federal, state, and local officials; and program administrators on factors that facilitate the use of promising approaches and that could broaden their use. We assessed information and communication HHS provides to states related to promising approaches against federal internal control standards.[4]

We obtained budget, performance, and other program data for the programs we selected, as well as HHS administrative data on states' engagement of TANF recipients in prescribed work activities. We assessed the reliability of these data by reviewing related documentation and interviewing knowledgeable officials and determined they were sufficiently reliable for providing contextual information on these programs and describing work participation trends, respectively. We also reviewed relevant GAO, HHS Office of Inspector General, and HHS reports, as well as relevant federal laws, regulations, and guidance.

We conducted this performance audit from January 2014 to November 2014 in accordance with generally accepted government auditing standards. Those standards require that we plan and perform the audit to obtain sufficient, appropriate evidence to provide a reasonable basis for our findings and conclusions based on our audit objectives. We believe that the evidence obtained provides a reasonable basis for our findings and conclusions based on our audit objectives.

Appendix II: Categories of Federal Work Activities and Limitations on Counting Time in Those Activities

In meeting the 30-hour average weekly requirement, individuals must spend at least 20 of the hours in certain activities (referred to as core activities). Any additional hours needed to meet the requirement can come from non-core or core activities.

Table 3. Categories of Federal Work Activities

Activity	Definition	At least daily supervision required	Limitations on counting time (for all families)
"Core" activities			
Unsubsidized employment	Full- or part-time employment in the public or private sector that is not subsidized by TANF or any other public program.		
Subsidized private sector employment	Employment in the private sector for which the employer receives a subsidy from TANF or other public funds to offset some or all of the wages and costs of employing an individual.		
Subsidized public sector employment	Employment in the public sector for which the employer receives a subsidy from TANF or other public funds to offset some or all of the wages and costs of employing an individual.		
Work experience	A work activity, performed in return for welfare, that provides an individual with an opportunity to acquire the general skills, knowledge, and work habits necessary to obtain employment. The purpose of work experience is to improve the employability of an individual who cannot find unsubsidized full-time employment.	X	

Activity	Definition	At least daily supervision required	Limitations on counting time (for all families)
On-the-job training	Training in the public or private sector that is given to a paid employee while he or she is engaged in productive work and that provides knowledge and skills essential to the full and adequate performance of the job.		
Job search and job readiness assistance	The act of seeking or obtaining employment, preparation to seek or obtain employment, including life-skills training, and substance abuse treatment, mental health treatment, or rehabilitation activities. Such treatment or therapy must be determined to be necessary and documented by a qualified medical, substance abuse, or mental health professional.	X	Participation in this activity may be counted for 6 weeks(12 weeks in certain circumstances) in a year
Community service programs	Structured programs and embedded activities in which individuals perform work for the direct benefit of the community under the auspices of public or nonprofit organizations. Community service programs must be limited to projects that serve a useful community purpose in fields such as health, social service, environmental protection, education, urban and rural redevelopment, welfare, recreation, public facilities, public safety, and child care.	X	

Table 3. (Continued)

Activity	Definition	At least daily supervision required	Limitations on counting time (for all families)
Vocational educational training	Organized educational programs that are directly related to the preparation of individuals for employment in current or emerging occupations.	X	Participation in this activity islimited to 12 months in an individual's lifetime
Caring for a child of a recipient in community service	Providing child care to enable another cash welfare recipient to participate in a community services program. This is an unpaid activity and must be a structured program designed to improve the employability of participating individuals.	X	
"Non-core" activities			
Job skills training directly related to employment	Training or education for job skills required by an employer to provide an individual with the ability to obtain employment or to advance or adapt to the changing demands of the workplace.	X	Must be combined with 20 hours per week in a "core" activity
Education directly related to employment (for those without a high school diploma or equivalent certificate)	Education related to a specific occupation, job, or job offer.	X	Must be combined with 20 hours per week in a "core" activity

Activity	Definition	At least daily supervision required	Limitations on counting time (for all families)
Attendance in a secondary school program or course of study leading to a certificate of general equivalence (for those who have not completed secondary school or gotten a certificate of general equivalence)	Regular attendance, in accordance with the requirements of a secondary school or course of study, at a secondary school or in a course of study leading to a certificate of general equivalence, in the case of a work-eligible individual who has not completed secondary school or received such a certificate.	X	Must be combined with 20 hours per week in a “core” activity

Source: GAO analysis of relevant federal laws and regulations. | GAO-15-31

APPENDIX III: SELECTED RECENT AND ONGOING DEPARTMENT OF HEALTH AND HUMAN SERVICES-FUNDED EVALUATIONS

Recent Studies

Employment Retention and Advancement Project (ERA): This study ran from 1998 to 2011. Under the study, Health and Human Services issued planning grants to 13 states to develop new programs. The goal was to test strategies for helping employed individuals keep their jobs and advance in the workforce. Only 3 of the programs were found to increase employment retention and advancement: the Texas sites (Corpus Christi and Fort Worth), Chicago, and Riverside PASS ERA programs. An ERA report was published in April 2010, “The Employment Retention and Advancement Project: How Effective Are Different Approaches Aiming to Increase Employment Retention and Advancement? Final Impacts for Twelve Models,” which can be viewed at: http://www.acf.hhs.gov/programs/opre/resource/the-employmentretention-and-advancement-project-how-effective-are. Among the participating sites, 8 were led by TANF agencies at either the state or local level. The Texas ERA program offered monthly stipends of $200 to former

TANF recipients working at least 30 hours per week. The Chicago program was a work-focused advancement program, offering targeted job search assistance and help indentifying and accessing career ladders. These services were provided to participants by staff in a private, for-profit firm, and TANF recipients were required to have regular contact with program staff to continue to receive TANF benefits. In contrast, the Riverside PASS ERA program provided voluntary, individualized retention and advancement services provided primarily by three community-based organizations and community colleges. Each of these programs targeted a specific population's service needs.

Enhanced Services for Hard-to-Employ Demonstrations and Evaluations: This demonstration tested several strategies for helping hard-to-employ parents find and sustain employment. One of the four sites in the study included TANF participants: the Transitional Work Corporation in Philadelphia conducted a subsidized employment demonstration exclusively for TANF clients. Other sites included programs in Kansas, Missouri, New York, Pennsylvania, and Rhode Island. This 10-year evaluation was completed in 2012. Findings from this study were used to influence the design of two new federal subsidized employment initiatives. Final evaluation reports can be viewed at: http://www.mdrc.org/publication/what-strategies-work-hard-employ.

Temporary Assistance for Needy Families/ Supplemental Security Income Disability Transition Project (TSDTP): This study is an effort to identify the extent of overlap between TANF and SSI programs and populations and develop pilot programs aimed to improve a variety of outcomes for individuals with disabilities and work-limiting barriers to employment. The study is a collaboration between ACF and the Social Security Administration through a contract with MDRC. This study is complete. Reports were published throughout 2013 and 2014. TSDTP included Ramsey County, Minnesota—a program highlighted in this GAO report—which participated in a pilot-phase experiment to increase employment among TANF participants with work limitations and disabilities. Los Angeles County, California and Muskegon County, Michigan were also involved in the study, implementing pilot tests of approaches to serving individuals with disabilities either through the provision of services to TANF participants with work-limiting barriers, streamlining the Supplemental Security Income application process, or improving coordination between the two systems.

Ongoing Studie

Behavioral Innovations to Increase Self-Sufficiency (BIAS) study: Launched in 2010, BIAS is the first major opportunity to apply a behavioral economics lens to programs that serve poor families in the United States. The goal of the study is to learn how tools from behavioral science can improve the well-being of low-income children, adults and families. The study is being conducted by OPRE and MDRC in partnership with behavioral experts. One site within the study is the Los Angeles county TANF agency. Results are planned for rolling release in 2014 and 2015. Two reports on BIAS were issued in April and August of 2014.

Health Professions Opportunities Grant (HPOG): HPOG was established by the Patient Protection and Affordable Care Act with the goal of providing training programs in high-demand healthcare professions to TANF recipients and other low-income individuals. In 2010, the Administration for Children and Families (ACF) awarded five-year grants to 32 grantees in 23 states. The program includes post-secondary educational institutions, workforce investment boards, state and local government agencies, and community-based organizations. Two of the 27 non-tribal HPOG grantees are Departments of Human or Social Services agencies and also administer the TANF program. One of the five tribal sites also administers the Tribal TANF program. However, a number of HPOG grantees also serve as the employment services providers for TANF agencies. ACF's Office of Planning, Research, and Evaluation (OPRE) is evaluating HPOG demonstration projects. An interim analysis of the impacts of HPOG is expected in June 2016.

Innovative Strategies for Increasing Self-Sufficient Project: The Innovative Strategies for Increasing Self-Sufficiency evaluation began in 2007 as a multi-site, random-assignment evaluation of promising strategies for increasing employment and self-sufficiency among low-income families. It is under the direction of ACF. This study focuses on the career pathways approach as the main intervention. One of the nine ISIS sites—Seattle/King County Workforce Development Corporation—is a contracted employment services provider for a local TANF agency and serves both TANF and non-TANF clients. Other sites in the study include: Des Moines Area Community College, I-BEST in Washington State, Instituto del Progreso Latino, Madison Area Technical College, Pima Community College, San Diego Workforce Partnership, and Valley Initiative for Development and Advancement.

Job Search Assistance (JSA) Strategies: This study was launched by OPRE in fall 2013 and features a multi-site, random-assignment evaluation to measure the relative impact of specific job search services offered by TANF programs on short-term labor market outcomes such as earnings and time to employment. The JSA evaluation aims (1) to provide information about the relative impacts of various JSA services and the manner in which agencies provide them, and (2) to provide actionable and policy-relevant feedback to the TANF field, including federal TANF policymakers, state and local TANF administrators, and frontline caseworkers. Site recruitment is ongoing, and initial findings could be reported as early as the end of 2016.

Subsidized and Transitional Employment Demonstration (STED): The STED study was launched by ACF in 2010 with the goal of demonstrating and evaluating the next generation of subsidized employment models for critical low-income populations. The project is led by MDRC, under contract with ACF, and examines strategies for providing counter-cyclical employment and for successfully transitioning individuals from short-term subsidized employment to unsubsidized employment. STED is being conducted in coordination with the Department of Labor's Enhanced Transitional Jobs Demonstration Project. Random assignment began at the first sites in early 2012 and continued through late 2013. Of the seven STED sites, three are TANF agency-operated including Los Angeles, San Francisco, and Minnesota. The evaluation is scheduled to run through 2017.

APPENDIX IV: BIBLIOGRAPHY

Bloom, Dan. *Transitional Jobs: Background, Program Models, and Evaluation Evidence*. Prepared by MDRC for the Department of Health and Human Services. Washington, D.C.: 2010.

———, Cynthia Miller, and Gilda Azurdia. *Results from the Personal Roads to Individual Development and Employment (PRIDE) Program in New York City*. MDRC. July 2007.

———, Pamela J. Loprest, and Sheila R. Zedlewski. *TANF Recipients with Barriers to Employment. Washington. D.C.: Urban Institute, August 2011.*

Derr, Michelle and LaDonna Pavetti. *Assisting TANF Recipients Living with Disabilities to Obtain and Maintain Employment: Creating Work Opportunities*. Prepared by Mathematica Policy Research, Inc. for the U.S. Department of Health and Human Services. Washington, D.C.: February 2008.

Greenberg, David H., Victoria Deitch, and Gayle Hamilton. "A Synthesis of Random Assignment Benefit-Cost Studies of Welfare-to-Work

Programs."*Journal of Benefit-Cost Analysis,* vol. 1, issue 1, article 3 (2010).

Gueron, Judith M. and Gayle Hamilton. *The Role of Education and Training in Welfare Reform.* The Brookings Institution, Policy Brief no. 20 (April 2002).

Hamilton, Gayle. *Improving Employment and Earnings for TANF Recipients.* Prepared by the Urban Institute for the Department of Health and Human Services. Washington, D.C.: March 2012.

———. *Moving People from Welfare to Work: Lessons from the National Evaluation of Welfare-to-Work Strategies.* Prepared by MDRC for the Department of Health and Human Services and Department of Education. Washington, D.C.: 2002.

Hendra, Richard, Keri-Nicole Dillman, Gayle Hamilton, Erika Lundquist, Karin Martinson, and Melissa Wavelet. *The Employment Advancement Project: How Effective Are Different Approaches Aiming to Increase Employment Retention and Advancement? Final Impacts for Twelve Models.* Prepared by MDRC for the Department of Health and Human Services. Washington, D.C.: April 2010.

Kirby, Gretchen, Heather Hill, LaDonna Pavetti, Jon Jacobson, Michelle Derr, and Pamela Winston. *Transitional Jobs: Stepping Stones to Unsubsidized Employment.* Washington, D.C.: Mathematica Policy Research, Inc., April 2002.

Maguire, Sheila, Joshua Freely, Carol Clymer, Maureen Conway, and Deena Schwartz. *Tuning In to Local Labor Markets: Findings from the Sectoral Employment Impact Study.* Philadelphia, PA: Public/Private Ventures, 2010.

Roder, Anne, and Mark Elliott. *Stimulating Opportunity: An Evaluation of ARRA-Funded Subsidized Employment Programs.* Economic Mobility Corporation, New York, NY: September 2013.

Werner, Alan, Catherine Dun Rappaport, Jennifer Bagnell Stuart, and Jennifer Lewis. *Literature Review: Career Pathways Programs,* OPRE Report #2013-24, Office of Planning, Research and Evaluation, Administration for Children and Families, U.S. Department of Health and Human Services (Washington, D.C.: June 24, 2013).

End Notes

[1] 42 U.S.C. § 601 et seq.

[2] Federal law governing TANF generally refers to the term "assistance" and does not make distinctions between different forms of aid funded by TANF. However, HHS draws distinctions between "assistance" and "nonassistance." HHS regulations define assistance to include cash, payments, vouchers, or other forms of benefits designed to meet families' ongoing, basic needs. 45 C.F.R. § 260.31. HHS also generally includes in assistance services, such as child care and transportation assistance for parents who are unemployed. HHS uses the term nonassistance to refer to TANF expenditures that fulfill one of the four TANF purposes, but do not meet this regulatory definition. In our report, we refer to HHS's definition of assistance as "cash assistance."

[3] Specifically, we primarily focused on studies that used a random assignment (experimental) research design. This type of design compares the outcomes for groups that were randomly assigned either to the treatment or to a nonparticipating control group before the intervention, in an effort to control for any systematic difference between the groups that could account for a difference in their outcomes. A difference in these groups' outcomes is believed to represent the program's impact.

[4] GAO, *Standards for Internal Control in the Federal Government*, GAO/AIMD-00-21.3.1 (Washington, D.C.: November 1999).

[5] Pub. L. No. 104-193, sec. 103(a)(1), § 401, 110 Stat. 2105, 2113.

[6] According to HHS, most states either have a shorter and more restrictive time limit, or use state funds or a hardship exemption to exempt or extend assistance to families.

[7] Pub. L. No. 104-193, § sec. 103(a)(1), § 403(b), 110 Stat. 2105, 2122. For example, collectively, states in economic distress can access up to $612 million in the TANF Contingency Fund in each of fiscal years 2013 and 2014, but they must spend more than a specified amount of state funds to do so.

[8] The work participation rate requirement for two-parent families is generally 90 percent.

[9] 42 U.S.C. § 607(b)(3).

[10] 45 C.F.R. § 261.43.

[11] See 64 Fed. Reg. 17,720, 17,722 (Apr. 12, 1999). Further, the Deficit Reduction Act of 2005, which reauthorized the TANF block grant, was generally expected to strengthen these work requirements by adding several provisions to improve the reliability of work participation data and program integrity and by modifying the caseload reduction credit.

[12] GAO, *Temporary Assistance for Needy Families: Implications of Recent Legislative and Economic Changes for State Programs and Work Participation Rates*, GAO-10-525 (Washington, D.C.: May 28, 2010).

[13] Pub. L. No. 111-291, § 812, 124 Stat. 3064, 3160.

[14] In fiscal year 2011, about 54 percent of families receiving cash assistance included an individual who was considered work-eligible for the purpose of the work participation rate. Work-eligible individuals are generally adult recipients of cash assistance or certain non-cash recipient parents of children receiving assistance, who count toward the work participation rate.

[15] HHS reported that the data from states indicate that individuals with zero hours of participation represent a range of situations including the following: individuals who are non-compliant and are in the sanction process; families disregarded from the participation rate because they were caring for a child under age one, subject to a work-related sanction, or

participating in a Tribal work program; individuals the state or local agency failed to engage; and individuals who were exempt due to illness or disability.

[16] In meeting the 30-hour average weekly requirement, individuals must spend at least 20 of the hours in certain activities (referred to as core activities). Any additional hours needed to meet the requirement can come from non-core or core activities. (See appendix II for the 12 categories of federal work activities and limitations on counting time in those activities.) Some activities have restrictions on the amount of time that can be spent in them and still be counted toward the work participation rate. For example, counting participation in job search and job readiness assistance is limited to no more than six weeks in a 12-month period (or 12 weeks in a 12-month period if the state meets the definition of a "needy state" for the TANF Contingency Fund) and no more than four consecutive weeks. Vocational educational training is limited to 12 months over an individual's lifetime, and no more than 30 percent of the families that a state counts toward its federal work participation rates may do so through participation in vocational educational training.

[17] AFDC and, subsequently, TANF, were authorized under the Social Security Act, as amended.

[18] States could claim the cost of evaluation as a regular AFDC expenditure and receive matching federal funding, according to HHS officials.

[19] Some members of Congress have raised concerns about a 2012 announcement by HHS that the agency would use waiver authority to allow states to test various strategies, policies, and procedures designed to improve employment outcomes for needy families. HHS made this announcement in a July 2012 Information Memorandum, Transmittal No. TANF-ACF-IM-2012-03. On September 4, 2012, we held that this Information Memorandum constitutes a rule and is subject to the Congressional Review Act's requirement that it be submitted to Congress and the Comptroller General before taking effect. See B-323772, Sept. 4, 2012. While questions have been raised about the extent of HHS's authority to take this action, neither this report nor our issued products, B323772, Sept. 4, 2012 or GAO-12-1028R, Sept. 19, 2012, address whether the Information Memorandum is a valid interpretation of statutes or regulations. The potential for waivers has been controversial and the House of Representatives passed a bill in 2013 aimed at preventing HHS from implementing them (*Preserving the Welfare Work Requirement and TANF Extension Act of 2013*, H.R. 890, 113th Cong. (2013)). This legislation has not been enacted. According to HHS, as of November 3, 2014, no state had formally submitted a request for a waiver related to TANF work requirements.

[20] 42 U.S.C. § 613(a).

[21] In this report, we focus on TANF cash assistance recipients.

[22] GAO, *Temporary Assistance for Needy Families: More Accountability Needed to Reflect Breadth of Block Grant Services,* GAO-13-33 (Washington, D.C.: Dec. 6, 2012).

[23] Generally, in child-only cases, the parent or adult caregiver is not eligible for benefits for one or more of a variety of reasons, such as receipt of certain other federal benefits or immigration status. See GAO, *TANF and Child Welfare Programs: Increased Data Sharing Could Improve Access to Benefits and Services*, GAO-12-2 (Washington, D.C.: Oct. 7, 2011).

[24] 64 Fed. Reg. 17,720, 17,722 (Apr. 12, 1999).

[25] See appendix IV for a bibliography.

[26] The New Deal's Works Progress Administration, which employed more than 8 million people in infrastructure projects in the 1930s, was an early subsidized employment program. See Dan Bloom, *Transitional Jobs: Background, Program Models, and Evaluation Evidence*, a

report prepared by MDRC at the request of U.S. Department of Health and Human Services, 2010.

[27] The AFDC Homemaker Home Health Aid demonstration produced increases in employment and earnings in most of the seven sites that were sustained for 3 years. *Transitional Jobs, 5.*

[28] The Center for Employment Opportunities and the Transitional Work Corporation, both part of the HHS Enhanced Services for the Hard-to-Employ project, generated decreases in recidivism and welfare receipt, respectively. The Center for Employment Opportunities program targeted former prisoners. Reductions in recidivism, relative to a control group, continued for program participants even after employment gains dissipated. According to the Center for Employment Opportunities evaluation, relationships with program staff or attitudinal changes resulting from program participation may have contributed to this reduction. Meanwhile, participants in the Transitional Work Corporation program experienced reductions in TANF receipt of about $600 per person over the first 18 months of the follow-up period. *Transitional Jobs, 26, 33, 35.*

[29] The American Recovery and Reinvestment Act of 2009 created a $5 billion Emergency Contingency Fund for state TANF programs, available in fiscal years 2009 and 2010. Pub. L. No. 111-5, § 2101(a)(1), 123 Stat. 115, 446.

[30] Anne Roder and Mark Elliott, Stimulating Opportunity: An Evaluation of ARRA-Funded Subsidized Employment Programs, Economic Mobility Corporation, Inc. (New York, NY: September 2013).

[31] *Stimulating Opportunity, 7.*

[32] This refers to the Personal Roads to Individual Development and Employment program. See Dan Bloom, Cynthia Miller, and Gilda Azurdia, *Results from the Personal Roads to Individual Development and Employment (PRIDE) Program in New York City*, a report prepared by MDRC at the request of the Department of Health and Human Services (July 2007).

[33] The Building Nebraska Families program produced significant increases in employment, earnings, and other outcomes for very hard-to-employ participants. See Dan Bloom, Pamela J. Loprest, and Sheila R. Zedlewski, *TANF Recipients with Barriers to Employment,* Urban Institute (Washington. D.C.: August 2011).

[34] See Administration for Children and Families, Department of Health and Human Services, "Executive Function Meeting of Experts," accessed August 6, 2014, http://www.acf.hhs.gov/opre-executive-function-meeting-of-experts.

[35] Sheila Maguire et al., *Tuning In to Local Labor Markets: Findings from the Sectoral Employment Impact Study,* Public/Private Ventures (Philadelphia, PA: 2010).

[36] Judith M. Gueron and Gayle Hamilton, "The Role of Education and Training in Welfare Reform," The Brookings Institution, Policy Brief no. 20 (April 2002).

[37] Although a comprehensive career pathways program has not yet been rigorously evaluated, we included this approach because it was based on a rigorous evaluation of sector-based career training and lessons from other prior rigorous evaluations.

[38] In a joint letter issued on April 4, 2012, the agencies defined career pathways as "a series of connected education and training strategies and support services that enable individuals to secure industry relevant certification and obtain employment within an occupational area and to advance to higher levels of future education and employment in that area." In addition, the Workforce Innovation and Opportunity Act makes several references to career pathways. For example, one purpose of the title of the Act dealing with adult education and literacy is to create partnerships to assist adults in the transition to postsecondary education and training, including through career pathways.

[39] 79 Fed. Reg. 22,662 (Apr. 23, 2014).

[40] Gayle Hamilton, *Moving People from Welfare to Work: Lessons from the National Evaluation of Welfare-to-Work Strategies,* a report prepared by Manpower Demonstration Research Corporation at the request of the Department of Education (Washington, D.C.: 2002).

[41] We did not review any state laws or regulations. All information on state laws or regulations was provided by state and local officials.

[42] Unforeseen circumstances, such as caring for a sick child, may cause a TANF recipient to miss a scheduled appointment or some hours of work activity. Some states use sanctions, such as a reduction in the amount of TANF cash assistance or gradual or immediate termination of TANF cash assistance, to encourage recipients to participate in program activities, according to one study.

[43] According to officials, California allows TANF recipients to participate in up to 24 months of education or training, even though only 12 months of vocational educational training is countable toward the federal work participation rate.

[44] GAO, *Standards for Internal Control in the Federal Government*, GAO/AIMD-00-21.3.1 (Washington, D.C.: November 1999).

[45] In 2010, the Departments of Labor and Education initiated a one-year Career Pathways Initiative that funded nine states and two tribal entities to develop sustainable career pathways and promote linkages among system partners. As part of the initiative, two Career Pathways Institutes brought together grantee teams and subject matter experts, state and local practitioners, and federal staff.

[46] In addition to federal TANF funds, selected programs reported receiving funds from state and local sources. However, some of these funds may have included federal TANF funds that were being allocated by state and local entities. In addition, some of these state or local funds may have been used by states to meet their TANF maintenance of effort requirement.

[47] Pub. L. No. 104-193, § 103(a)(1), 110 Stat. 2105, 2112.

[48] 42 U.S.C. §§ 601(a), 617. Accordingly, HHS has limited authority to influence state program choices and cannot compel states to adopt particular approaches for their welfare-to-work programs.

[49] 42 U.S.C. §§ 601(a), 604(a).

[50] In this report, we concluded that while states still spend some portion of TANF funds on welfare-to-work programs for the cash assistance population, their new and varied uses of TANF funds for non-cash services over time beyond this population raise questions about how state efforts are contributing to TANF purposes. We recommended that HHS develop a plan for revising its financial reporting categories to better understand how states use TANF funds. HHS subsequently published an information memorandum and Federal Register notices on a revised reporting form for collecting more detailed and accurate TANF expenditure data. See 78 Fed. Reg. 56,236 (Sept. 12, 2013), 79 Fed. Reg. 2444 (Jan. 14, 2014). The agency said it plans to implement the revised form in fiscal year 2015 and provide technical assistance to states through this transition. GAO, *Temporary Assistance for Needy Families: More Accountability Needed to Reflect Breadth of Block Grant Services*, GAO-13-33, (Washington, D.C.: Dec. 6, 2012).

[51] See 42 U.S.C. § 607(c).

[52] See 42 U.S.C. § 607(c).

[53] In 2010, we reported that some states have opted to fund cash assistance for certain low-income families with state dollars not counted toward the state's maintenance of effort requirement, known as solely state funds. Families provided with cash assistance through solely state funds are not included in the work participation rate calculation. We reported

that families for whom states use solely state funds to provide cash assistance are those that typically have the most difficulty meeting the TANF work requirements, such as families that included a parent with disabilities. See *Temporary Assistance for Needy Families: Implications of Recent Legislative and Economic Changes for State Programs and Work Participation Rates*, GAO-10-525 (Washington, D.C.: May 28, 2010). According to HHS, families in a solely state funded program are not in the numerator or denominator used to calculate the work participation rate, but they could affect the calculation of the caseload reduction credit because any such shift would be considered an eligibility change. A reduced caseload due to an eligibility policy change does not count toward a caseload reduction credit.

[54] As of our 2010 report, for which we surveyed all 50 states and the District of Columbia, 14 states provided cash assistance to low-income families with significant barriers to employment using solely state funds. The report found that in 9 of these 14 states, work participation rules were generally not the same for these families as for families in the state's TANF program. We did not collect information on what employment services, if any, are provided to these families.

[55] See 42 U.S.C. § 607(d)(8).

[56] GAO-10-525 and *Temporary Assistance for Needy Families: Update on Families Served and Work Participation,* GAO-11-880T (Washington, D.C.: Sept. 8, 2011).

[57] In this report, we identified a number of potential options that could improve TANF performance and oversight, based on our prior work, and that might be considered as part of an extension or reauthorization of TANF. GAO, *Temporary Assistance for Needy Families: Potential Options to Improve Performance and Oversight*, GAO-13-431 (Washington, D.C.: May 15, 2013).

[58] These programs are participating or have participated in rigorous impact evaluations sponsored by HHS. The Los Angeles County subsidized employment program and nonTANF clients in San Francisco Jobs Now! are being included in the Subsidized and Transitional Employment Demonstration. Washington's I-BEST is part of the Innovative Strategies for Increasing Self-Sufficiency project. Ramsey County's FAST program was evaluated as part of the TANF/Supplemental Security Income Disability Transition Project. For more information on these studies, see Appendix III.

[59] In our prior work, we have noted that the ethical concern that the control group should not be harmed by withholding needed services can be addressed by providing the control group with whatever services are considered standard practice. In this case, however, the evaluation will no longer be testing whether a new approach is effective *at all*; it will instead test whether it is more effective than standard practice. GAO, *Program Evaluation: A Variety of Rigorous Methods Can Help Identify Effective Interventions*, GAO-10-30 (Washington, D.C.: Nov. 23, 2009).

[60] GAO, *Welfare Reform: More Information Needed to Assess Promising Strategies to Increase Parents' Incomes*, GAO-06-108 (Washington, D.C.: Dec. 2, 2005).

[61] One of the sites was a nonprofit that conducted a program exclusively for TANF clients.

[62] According to HHS, in preliminary analysis for the Innovative Strategies for Increasing Self-Sufficiency evaluation approximately 14 percent of all sample members were receiving TANF at baseline, with a high of nearly 40 percent in one site. In preliminary analysis for the Health Profession Opportunity Grants evaluation, similarly, 15 percent of participants were receiving TANF, with a number of sites reporting a quarter or more as being TANF recipients.

End Notes for Appendix I

[1] Research shows that welfare-to-work programs that increase employment and earnings do not necessarily increase household incomes. This is because the increased income from earnings can be offset by the loss of cash welfare, food stamps, and other support services.

[2] GAO, *Program Evaluation: A Variety of Rigorous Methods Can Help Identify Effective Interventions,* GAO-10-30 (Washington, D.C.: Nov. 23, 2009).

[3] According to HHS, the majority of states centrally administer TANF, but some states (California, Colorado, Minnesota, New Jersey, New York, North Dakota, Ohio, and Wisconsin) play a supervisory role and delegate administration of TANF to the counties.

[4] GAO, *Standards for Internal Control in the Federal Government*, GAO/AIMD-00-21.3.1 (Washington, D.C.: November 1999).

In: Temporary Assistance for Needy Families ISBN: 978-1-63482-612-9
Editor: Salvatore Hoffman

Chapter 2

TEMPORARY ASSISTANCE FOR NEEDY FAMILIES (TANF): WELFARE-TO-WORK REVISITED*

Gene Falk

SUMMARY

One of the central features of the Temporary Assistance for Needy Families (TANF) block grant is promoting work and job preparation for parents (mostly single mothers) in families that receive cash assistance. TANF was created in the 1996 welfare law, which was the culmination of a decades-long evolution from providing single mothers "pensions" to permit them to stay home and raise children to a program focused on work. State TANF programs were influenced by research conducted during a period of much experimentation on welfare-to-work initiatives in the 1980s and early 1990s, which found that mandatory work requirements could reduce welfare receipt and increase employment among single mothers.

TANF aids some of the most disadvantaged families with children. These families are in a wide range of circumstances, and some of them are not subject to state welfare-to-work efforts. In FY2011, about 6 in 10 TANF assistance families had "work-eligible" individuals. TANF work-eligible individuals comprise in great part single mothers with young

---

* This is an edited, reformatted and augmented version of a Congressional Research Service publication, No. R42767, dated September 11, 2014.

children. In FY2011, about a third of TANF work-eligible mothers were young (under the age of 24). Additionally, 40% of all work-eligible women lacked a high school diploma or the equivalent.

As a block grant to the states, TANF sets federal goals such as ending dependence of needy parents on government through work and job preparation, gives states flexibility in program design to achieve those goals, and measures the performance of states. The work requirements that actually apply to recipients are determined by the states, not by federal rules. In FY2011, 42% (monthly average) of all work-eligible adults were either working or engaged in a job preparation activity. The most common activity was working in a job while remaining on the rolls. Job search and vocational educational training followed as the second and third most common activities.

While state rules—not federal rules—determine work requirements for individual TANF recipients, federal TANF law establishes work participation standards that apply to the states and influence state program designs. The federal work standards are performance measures used to assess state TANF welfare-to-work efforts. The federal TANF work standards set target participation rates, specify activities that can be counted toward meeting the standards, and set minimum hours of engagement per week in a month for a recipient to be considered engaged in countable activities. The target participation rates vary by state: the statute sets a 50% standard for all families, but the standard is reduced by credits states may earn for caseload reduction. In FY2011, the official TANF work participation *rate* was 29.5%; however, all but seven states, the District of Columbia, and Guam met their all-family work *standard*.

The TANF work standards date back to the 1996 law, and reflect the policy concerns and the research on welfare-to-work programs of the time. Research on new welfare-to-work models since the 1996 law has yielded mixed and limited results. However, some innovations in workforce and education programs have yet to be tested within a welfare-to-work context. Policy makers also face questions about whether the sole focus of the assessment of TANF's success ought to be welfare-to-work. TANF has evolved into a program where cash assistance represents less than 30% of its funds. Policy makers thus face questions of whether consideration might be given to developing measures and assessment of how well TANF does in meeting other goals related to improving the circumstances of families with children.

INTRODUCTION

One of the central features of the 1996 welfare reform law (Personal Responsibility and Work Opportunity Reconciliation Act of 1996, PRWORA,

P.L. 104-193) was its focus on requiring and promoting work and job preparation for parents (mostly single mothers) in needy families with children. That law created the Temporary Assistance for Needy Families (TANF) block grant, and completed a decades-long evolution in policy, from one where cash assistance was provided to families headed by single mothers to permit them to stay at home and care for their children to one of encouraging and ultimately requiring work.

It is sometimes said that TANF requires adult recipients to work in exchange for their family's cash assistance. However, this is not what federal law says. In any given month, many recipients work or are engaged in work-related activities; however, many are not so engaged. TANF establishes numerical work participation performance standards that apply to a state's total caseload, not individual recipients, and leaves to states the decision about how to meet those standards. It is the states that determine who is required to work or participate in activities. It is also the states that determine the activities that meet an individual recipient's work requirements.

TANF's work rules generally date back to the 1996 welfare reform law, which was enacted following a period of growth in the welfare rolls. Cash assistance caseloads increased greatly from 1960 through the mid-1970s, ushering in a period of debate about "welfare reform." The caseloads again began to increase in the very late 1980s, reaching a peak of 5.1 million families on the rolls in March 1994. Discussion of TANF work rules today is in a different context than occurred in the late 1980s or early 1990s. The cash assistance rolls diminished greatly, and stood at 1.9 million families in FY2011. In any given month in FY2011, state TANF welfare-to-work efforts could touch a population of about 1.3 million adults.

This report examines the work participation standards and requirements for cash assistance recipients of the TANF block grant, which was created in the 1996 welfare reform law. This report

- provides a short history of work requirements in programs that provide cash assistance to needy families with children;
- reviews the major studies that contribute to the knowledge of what types of welfare-to-work programs are effective;
- discusses the TANF work provisions that apply directly to individuals and analyzes FY2011 data on engagement in work and work-related activities of adults in TANF households;

- discusses the TANF work participation standards that apply to states and analyzes FY2011 data on participation as they relate to those standards; and
- discusses some issues that Congress might consider in the future, such as how the work standards can address changing circumstances and the difficulties of measuring the performance of states in the context of a block grant.

BRIEF HISTORY: WORK REQUIREMENTS AND CASH AID FOR NEEDY FAMILIES WITH CHILDREN

In the early 20th century, prior to the enactment of a federal cash-in-aid program for families caring for dependent children in their own homes, many states had laws providing aid to mothers with dependent children, often called "mothers' pensions."[1] The general purpose of these pensions was summarized by a 1914 report published by the then-newly created Children's Bureau (then operating under the U.S. Department of Labor), which described the basic function of the various state pension laws as "preventing the breaking up of the home when on account of death or disability the support of the natural breadwinner of the family is removed."[2] By 1921, 40 states and the then-territories of Alaska and Hawaii had laws providing support for children in their own homes.[3] The intended recipients were, for the most part, widows and women whose husbands were disabled, were imprisoned, or had deserted the family. However, restrictions on eligibility varied by state and in some cases only widows were eligible.[4]

Limited state budgets meant that in many cases these early programs operated only partially or not at all. A Missouri law of 1911 applied only to Kansas City and limited expenditures for all pensions to $12,000 annually. In cases where funds were insufficient, a juvenile court would select "the most urgent cases" to receive pensions.[5]

The Great Depression exacerbated the degree to which counties dropped or downsized their programs, and by 1935 the number of families eligible for such aid under state laws was three times greater than the number of families actually receiving it.6, [7] Concern over the lack of sufficient support under state programs, as well as an increase in demand for financial help as a result of the Great Depression, prompted President Franklin D. Roosevelt to establish by Executive Order the Committee on Economic Security (CES) in 1934 to serve the broader purpose of "[providing] at once security against several of the great disturbing factors in life." Within six months, the CES had designed a proposal for the nation's first comprehensive federal social insurance program, which included aid to "children deprived of a father's support." In their report to the President in January 1935, the CES urged the creation of federal grants-in-aid to

> release from the wage-earning role the person whose natural function is to give her children the physical and affectionate guardianship necessary not alone to keep them from falling into social misfortune, but more affirmatively to rear them into citizens capable of contributing to society.[8]

In essence, the committee was proposing a program to provide mothers with the financial assistance necessary to remain at home with their children.

Later that year, following the recommendations of the CES, the Aid to Dependent Children program (ADC) was established as a federal grant-in-aid program to states to help them fund cash assistance to needy families with children. Authorized under the Social Security Act of 1935 (P.L. 74-271; H.R. 7260), ADC grants provided assistance to children under the age of 16 who had "been deprived of parental support or care by reason of death, continued absence from the home, or physical or mental incapacity of a parent." Cash benefits provided under ADC were primarily intended to enable mothers (typically widows) to stay at home and rear children. Echoing the sentiment voiced in the CES report to the President, the House Report accompanying H.R. 7260 stated that these benefits were to assist in aiding the families on relief who were "without a potential breadwinner other than a mother whose time might best be devoted to the care of her young children."[9]

Over the coming decades, the demography of ADC recipients began to change. Some of this change reflects changing demographics in the general population, such as the increase in female-headed families headed by divorced, separated, or never-married mothers as opposed to widows. Also affecting the demography of the ADC caseload was Social Security policy changes. At the program's onset, the most common ADC family was headed by a widow. Social Security benefits to widows, widowers, and child survivors were created in the Social Security Amendments of 1939, and those receiving ADC increasingly were families where the father was alive but absent. By 1942, the proportion of ADC families with women who were divorced, separated, or unmarried was about equal to the proportion of women who were widows. The caseload also became increasingly nonwhite.[10]

Though federal policy documents connected with the establishment of ADC stressed child-rearing as the policy rationale for providing aid, the expectations for work among low-income women may have differed at the state level. Some states adopted rules barring "employable" mothers from aid.[11]

Additionally, in the last half of the 20th Century, female participation in the workforce was on the rise, as norms for middle-class mothers changed with respect to child-rearing and work.[12] The assumption that women should remain in the home with their children began to diminish.[13]

The 1950s ushered in an increased focus on the self-sufficiency and rehabilitation of public aid recipients, and amendments to the ADC law began to reflect this reorientation. In 1956, the law (P.L. 84-880; H.R. 7225) was amended to include the provision that its purpose was to not only provide financial assistance to needy families with children, but also "to help such parents or relatives to attain the maximum self-support and personal independence consistent with the maintenance of continuing parental care and protection." The Senate Finance Committee Report accompanying H.R. 7225 further explained that "[s]ervices that assist families and individuals to attain the maximum economic and personal independence of which they are capable provide a more satisfactory way of living for the recipients affected."[14] The 1956 amendments also added Disability Insurance to the Social Security program, again potentially aiding some families that might otherwise rely on ADC for benefits.

With the advent of the 1960s, the focus on self-sufficiency progressed from symbolic statements and funding for services to actual federal program requirements. At first, however, these requirements focused on men when cash assistance was extended to families with two able-bodied parents with one unemployed. In 1961, in the midst of a recession and high unemployment, President Kennedy called on Congress to amend the ADC program to include the children of the unemployed.[15] That year, the law was changed to temporarily extend eligibility for ADC to dependent children of unemployed parents. For a state to provide assistance to families on the basis of unemployment, they were required to include in their state plan provisions for ensuring that the unemployed parent was registered for job placement services. If the parent refused to accept employment without "good cause" (as determined by the state), the state was required to halt assistance to the family.[16] For the first time since the program's inception, ADC now had the beginnings of federally mandated work requirements for families receiving assistance.

Continuing in this vein of promoting self-sufficiency, President Kennedy's speech to Congress the next year emphasized a shift toward favoring services over cash assistance. Public welfare, he stated, "must be directed increasingly toward prevention and rehabilitation ... we must place more stress on services instead of relief."[17] Also in 1962, the name of the program was changed to Aid to *Families* with Dependent Children (AFDC) to reflect the enlarged focus of the program and to emphasize the maintenance of two-parent families.[18]

The Social Security Amendments of 1967 (P.L. 90-248) enacted both financial incentives for adult recipients to work and, for the first time, requirements for AFDC mothers to work. These amendments required states to disregard from a family's countable income some earnings when determining its "need" and benefits.[19] They also created the first work program under AFDC—the Work Incentive Program (WIN). WIN was compulsory for fathers, and states could determine whether it would be compulsory or voluntary for mothers. In practice, two-thirds of participants in the WIN program between 1968 and 1971 were mothers. In 1971, the federal rules changed to require *all* parents to enroll in WIN, with the exception of mothers with children under the age of six.[20]

AFDC work requirements continued to evolve in the 1980s. The Omnibus Budget Reconciliation Act of 1981 (P.L. 97-35) gave states the option to require "workfare" (unpaid work in exchange for cash assistance) through Community Work Experience Programs (CWEP). The Family Support Act of 1988 (P.L. 100-485) ended WIN, replacing it with the Job Opportunity and Basic Skills (JOBS) Training Program. It was designed to provide AFDC recipients either job training and education or the quick acquisition of a job.[21] It also removed the participation exemption for many single parents by lowering the age-of-youngest-child exemption from six to three years (at state option, this could be lowered further to one year), while also increasing funding for child care. Significantly, JOBS legislated minimum participation rates for states in order to be eligible for their full federal fund allotment.[22] The program also placed an increased focus on education, as evidenced by the requirement that states offer education to any adult lacking a high school diploma and the provision of federal funding for such activities.[23]

The progression of welfare from a cash assistance-based program to one of work incentives, requirements, and supports culminated in the mid-1990s with welfare reform. With the signing of the Personal Responsibility and Work Opportunity Reconciliation Act of 1996 (P.L. 104-193), AFDC was replaced by the Temporary Assistance for Needy Families program. TANF instituted a range of work-related requirements that apply to both states and recipients. These requirements, and the extent to which they are being met, will be discussed below.

Welfare Reform and Research on Welfare, Dependency, and Work

Welfare was the subject of a great deal of research from the 1960s through the 1990s. Economic theory suggested that providing assistance without work reduces work effort, and a fairly large number of empirical studies supported that contention.[24]

Additionally, proposals to replace the existing welfare system with a negative income tax (with a minimum guaranteed income) was the subject of some of the first large-scale social experiments beginning in the 1960s and continuing into the 1980s. These experiments found that such policies reduced work effort and potentially even led to an increase in marital dissolutions.[25] The negative income tax with an income guarantee was offered as welfare reform during the Nixon and Carter administrations, but not thereafter.[26]

TANF was influenced by two major types of research published in the 1980s and early 1990s. The first was analyses of how long families remained on welfare. The second was a series of experimental evaluations of welfare-to-work initiatives: programs that offered employment services and education or training that encouraged participation, required participation, or did a combination of both.

Research on the Duration of Welfare Receipt

Beginning in the 1980s, research began to examine how long families remained on the rolls based on data that permitted examination of an individual's program receipt over time. A study conducted by Mary Jo Bane and David Ellwood prepared for HHS concluded that while most periods of welfare receipt are short, some families stay on the rolls for a long period of time.[27] Subsequent studies generally confirmed the basic findings of Bane's and Ellwood's initial report. Additionally, some recipients experienced multiple periods of benefit receipt. In a subsequent study, Ellwood found that close to one-fourth of those who ever come on to the welfare rolls would receive benefits for 10 years or more in their lifetime.[28]

Long-term benefit receipt raised concerns about welfare dependency. That is, there was concern that for some families, receipt of welfare had essentially become a way of life rather than a short-term means of coping with events such as job loss or marital dissolution.

Pre-1996 Welfare-to-Work Experiments[29]

The 1980s also saw welfare-to-work programs evaluated using random-assignment "social experiments" to test whether there were effective programs to move recipients from welfare to work.[30] Early studies focused on whether mandatory, relatively low-cost programs could affect the behavior of cash welfare recipients. The evaluations found that such programs that require mandatory participation can have positive impacts.[31] Most of these programs emphasized job search. Evaluated unpaid work experience programs (e.g., "workfare") tended to produce little in the way of positive employment impacts or reductions in welfare receipt, though the activity itself had value in providing services to the public at large.[32]

The period between the enactment of the Family Support Act of 1988 and PRWORA in 1996 saw a surge in experimentation on welfare-to-work approaches. In addition to authorizing the JOBS program itself, the Family Support Act of 1988 also authorized the study that would examine the impact of 11 mandatory welfare-to-work programs operating in seven sites. This major, eight-year study would come to be known as the National Evaluation of Welfare-to-Work Strategies (NEWWS). NEWWS studied the impact on welfare recipients and their children of these programs that took different approaches to getting recipients into work.

In addition to NEWWS, a number of states conducted evaluations of their own initiatives. These evaluations were a condition of states receiving "waivers" under Section 1115 of the Social Security Act. The key initiatives that influenced welfare reform and the design of state TANF programs were waiver programs that allowed recipients who went to work at low-paying jobs to remain on the rolls and supplement their earnings with a reduced welfare benefit, restricted the period of time families could receive benefits (time limits), and enhanced sanctions for those who failed to comply with program requirements. These "waiver" programs often became the basis for states' post-1996 TANF cash assistance programs.

GAIN—Riverside (California)

An early, influential set of welfare-to-work experiments was conducted on California's GAIN (Greater Avenues of Independence) program.[33] The GAIN program was evaluated in six counties, one of which was Riverside. The evaluation studied recipients who entered the GAIN program between 1988 and mid-1990.

Like other counties' GAIN programs, Riverside placed a heavy emphasis on skill-building services—about 60% of participants entered an education or training activity—but also maintained a strong focus on employment. Among the findings for each of the six counties, Riverside's program was the least costly to operate and generated the largest return for taxpayers. Over the three-year period in which it operated, Riverside's program increased the experimental group's earnings by an average of $3,113—a 49% gain over the control group average.

The National Evaluation of Welfare-to-Work Strategies (NEWWS)

The NEWWS evaluation studied impacts for those who entered its programs from mid-1991 through the end of 1994. The overall results of the NEWWS evaluations showed that mandatory participation in work or job preparation activities was likely to increase the amount of work recipients participated in and reduce the amount of welfare they received.[34] However, the requirements alone were not likely to raise incomes.

A key feature of NEWWS was its evaluation of different types of welfare-to-work strategies. In three locations—Atlanta, GA, Grand Rapids, MI, and Riverside, CA—programs based on job search, known as labor force attachment programs, were tested "head-to-head" against programs that provided more long-term education. In each location, *both* the labor force attachment and the education-focused programs produced positive impacts. Both types of programs raised employment and reduced welfare receipt.

However, when impacts are compared over a relatively long period (five years), the labor force attachment programs produced some larger impacts than the education-focused programs. This was particularly true for those without a high school diploma, as the labor force attachment programs increased employment rates more than the education-focused program in this subgroup over five years.

A separate analysis of NEWWS adult basic education activities, such as adult basic skills courses, pursuit of the General Educational Development (GED) credential, high school completion programs, and English as a Second Language (ESL), was published. In general, participation in these activities did not yield positive employment impacts. That study found that the programs attended by recipients of cash assistance often were not modified to account for the specific needs of students, and most participants failed to actually receive a GED. However, some positive impacts were found for the few who did go on to post-secondary education after receiving a GED.[35]

The program with the largest impacts in the NEWWS evaluation was the one operated in Portland, OR. That program was referred to as a "mixed" program model. It emphasized employment as a goal, but also permitted caseworkers the discretion to assign participants to education if warranted. Further, Portland's program emphasized finding a "good job," not just any job, and permitted extended job search.

While NEWWS included programs that were successful in raising employment rates and earnings and reducing welfare receipt, none—even the program with the largest positive impacts in Portland—succeeded in raising incomes. That is, increased earnings from work offset, but did not exceed, reductions in cash welfare and food assistance. Mandatory work requirements alone could increase work—but not necessarily the income of adult recipients and their children.

Earnings Supplement Programs

Several programs tested in the 1990s combined mandatory work participation with a policy that allowed recipients who went to work to remain on the rolls at higher levels of earnings or for longer periods of time than allowed under regular pre-1996 welfare law. This was seen as increasing financial incentives to work. One program—Minnesota's Family Investment Program or MFIP—also regarded this approach as a way to increase incomes and reduce poverty.[36]

The earnings supplement programs were generally successful in increasing work and raising incomes.[37] The MFIP program also examined the impact of being in the program on various measures of child development. It found some positive impacts in that domain as well. However, the increased income and positive child impacts came at a cost—the budget cost of additional welfare payments that supplemented earnings.

New Hope

The New Hope program was conducted in Milwaukee, WI, and existed from 1994 through 1998. It was available to adults living in one of two targeted neighborhoods who had a household income at or below 150% of the poverty line (it was the only program that did not limit participation to adults with children). The evaluators of New Hope described the program's philosophy:

> Four principles underlie the New Hope program: (1) that people who are willing and able to work full time should be assured the opportunity to do so; (2) that people who work full time should not be poor; (3) that people who work more hours should take home more pay; and (4) for those eligible for public assistance, that full-time work should make people better off financially than they would be on welfare. These principles are realized by providing four benefits and services to participants who are willing to work an average of at least 30 hours per week: help in obtaining a job (including access to a CSJ [Community Service Job] if full-time employment is not otherwise available), an earnings supplement to bring low-wage workers' income above the poverty level, subsidized health insurance, and subsidized child care.[38]

Participants were expected to work at least 30 hours per week, and the program provided a two-part income supplement—the first part was based on the number of children in the family, and the second was based on the participant's earnings. The program also supported work by including health benefits and child care assistance.

Additionally, New Hope offered unemployed recipients the opportunity to apply for a community service job in a nonprofit organization. These jobs paid the minimum wage, and allowed participants to also receive federal and Wisconsin earned income tax credits.

The New Hope evaluation program found that, after two years, the program increased earnings and employment for those who were not working full-time when they entered the program. It also resulted in a modest increase in income during the first two years. The increase in income was also accompanied by some positive impacts on the development of the children of participants. The evaluation also found that subsidized community service employment played a central role in New Hope. After New Hope ended, participants still experienced reduced poverty at five years after having entered the program, though impacts had faded by eight years after a recipient entered the program.

New Hope was a far broader program than merely a welfare-to-work program, and many of its features are reflected in the broader changes in low-income assistance that took place in the mid-1990s. TANF and welfare reform were a part of a series of changes to low-income assistance programs that expanded earnings supplements to "make work pay" through the Earned

Income Tax Credit (EITC), increased funding for subsidized child care, and expanded health insurance coverage through the creation of the Children's Health Insurance Program (CHIP) in 1997 and ultimately the Affordable Care Act of 2010.[39]

However, the current system of aid to low-income families lacks several elements of New Hope. One such element is the emphasis on full-time work. Another element the current system has generally lacked is publically-funded community services jobs when other jobs are not available—except for a brief period when extra TANF funds were available under the American Recovery and Reinvestment Act of 2009 (P.L. 111-5). (Subsidized employment under ARRA is discussed later in this report.) The system lacks such publically-funded community service jobs even though TANF funds may be used for them.

Post-Welfare Reform Research

The years immediately after the enactment of the 1996 welfare reform law saw a continuation of a high volume of research about cash assistance and its recipients. With the rapid decline in the cash assistance caseload, states examined the circumstances of those who left the rolls. Additionally, HHS continued to fund a series of experimental studies examining program innovations aimed at improving the impact of welfare-to-work programs on participants' employment and well-being.

Welfare "Leaver" Studies

Welfare "leaver" studies examined the circumstances of those who left the rolls: to what extent were they working, what were they earning, what other types of government benefits did they receive, and did they come back to the assistance rolls. A large number of these studies were conducted by the states using varying methodologies. Congress provided special funding to study the effects of welfare reform, and HHS used these funds to award grants to states and counties to conduct a set of studies using more consistent research methods.

A synthesis of the HHS leaver studies generally confirmed what had been found in the state-developed leaver studies:[40]

- The majority of those who leave welfare do so for work. Among the 15 states and localities examined in the HHS leaver studies, the "median study"—the midpoint of the ranking of all 15 studies—showed 57% of its leavers employed in the first quarter after exiting the rolls. Employment rates tended to remain fairly constant when examining the second, third, and fourth quarters after exit.

- Though most work after leaving the rolls, most studies report that only between 30% and 40% of those who left the welfare rolls worked in all four quarters after leaving welfare.
- Because not all welfare leavers find work or steady work, some of those who exit the rolls return to welfare. In the fourth quarter after leaving welfare, many of the states and localities reported that about one-fifth (20%) of their leavers had returned to the rolls.

Experimental Studies

Follow-up studies to the welfare-to-work experiments of the 1980s and 1990s have yielded mixed results on new initiatives to improve program impacts. HHS launched six multi-site experimental studies to examine additional program approaches for the cash assistance and related populations. Two of these studies are complete, with four studies planned or currently underway (with results forthcoming).

The Employment Retention and Advancement (ERA) Project: 1998-2011

The Employment Retention and Advancement (ERA) project sought to build on the knowledge of how to move welfare recipients into jobs by testing initiatives to improve impacts by increasing employment stability and advancement.[41] It provided some additional evidence that providing earnings supplements combined with employment services could result in positive earning impacts, including employment retention. ERA also produced some evidence that community-based organizations or for-profit providers of employment services could also produce positive employment impacts.

ERA also tested programs that combined work with education for those on the rolls. Those programs did not produce positive employment impacts.

The Hard-to-Serve: 2001-2012

Several ERA sites, as well as sites in a second experimental study, focused on populations that were hard to serve.[42] Some of these programs were not geared to the TANF cash assistance population, but rather, other disadvantaged groups (e.g., those leaving prison—who tended to be men). Programs that tested approaches such as subsidized "transitional jobs" provided both income boosts and employment to participants while they were in subsidized jobs, but there were no long-term impacts from program participation on employment or earnings.

A program in New York City that focused on those with cash assistance recipients who had limiting disabilities found positive earnings impacts and reduced cash assistance. However, employment rates for those in that program were below those in the general cash assistance population, and evaluators attributed much of the reduction in cash assistance to a high rate of sanctioning in the program.

Current Experimental Evaluations

HHS is fielding four additional experimental studies that at least partially focus on TANF assistance recipients or related populations that have yet to yield impact findings. The Innovative Strategies for Increasing Self-Sufficiency Project (ISISS) will test the "career pathways" model that seeks to move participants into better paying jobs within a sector through combining work and training. The Health Professions Opportunity Grant (HPOG) evaluation is measuring the impact of a program intended to provide career pathways within the health care sector. HPOG was created in the Affordable Care Act of 2010 (ACA, P.L. 111-148) with TANF cash assistance recipients and other low-income individuals as its target population. The Subsidized and Transitional Employment Demonstration (STED) examines subsidized employment models. The Job Search Assistance (JSA) strategies project is intended to measure the relative impact of differing job search services offered through TANF programs.

TANF WELFARE-TO-WORK PROVISIONS

TANF was created by the 1996 welfare reform law (the Personal Responsibility and Work Opportunity Reconciliation Act of 1996, P.L. 104-193). On the eve of that law's enactment, federal law already had in place rules requiring mandatory participation in welfare-to-work activities for some recipients. Aid to Families with Dependent Children required certain recipients to participate in activities, and it had a sanction for those who failed to participate.[43] States were also subject to participation standards. Many states had already gone further than federal law in requiring work of more recipients, increasing sanctions for noncompliance, and fashioning their own welfare-to-work approaches under "waivers" of AFDC federal rules. The Clinton

Administration granted welfare waivers to 43 states.[44] Thus, though ending AFDC and creating TANF was a major change in social policy, the welfare-to-work aspects of TANF represent a step in the evolution of welfare-to-work policies.

TANF is a broad-based block grant that provides funds to states, the territories, and Indian tribes to help them finance cash welfare programs for needy families with children as well as provide a wide range of other benefits and services to either ameliorate the effects or address the root causes of child poverty. The basic federal block grant for the 50 states and District of Columbia is funded at a total of $16.5 billion per year. States are required, under a provision known as the maintenance of effort (MOE) requirement, to expend from their own funds a minimum total of $10.4 billion per year in addition to federal funds on TANF or TANF-related programs.

The statutory purpose of TANF is to increase state flexibility to achieve the following goals:

1) provide assistance to needy families so that children may be cared for in their own homes or in the homes of relatives;
2) end the dependence of needy parents on government benefits by promoting job preparation, work, and marriage;
3) prevent and reduce the incidence of out-of-wedlock pregnancies and establish annual numerical goals for preventing and reducing the incidence of these pregnancies; and
4) encourage the formation and maintenance of two-parent families.

Though the block grant is a set amount, states may use TANF funds to finance any activity "reasonably calculated" to achieve any of these four TANF goals. This gives states broad leeway in spending TANF funds. In general, state MOE funds can be used for these same activities (there are some technical differences in the use of federal and state funds).

States determine the size of TANF benefits, and there is a wide range of benefit amounts among the states. In July 2011, the maximum monthly benefit for a family of three varied from $923 per month in Alaska and $788 per month in New York City to $170 in Mississippi. TANF has a five-year time limit on receipt of cash assistance financed by federal funds. Recipients of cash assistance also must cooperate in having their children's paternity established and other requirements relating to enforcement of child support orders.

TANF funds may be used to support work in various ways, including through helping states finance tax credits for low-income working families, providing assistance with transportation, and funding child care. TANF funds may supplement those from a separate child care block grant as TANF funds may be transferred to the child care block grant or spent within TANF itself on child care.[45]

Cash welfare itself accounted for less than 30% of all TANF and MOE funds in FY2011. The cash welfare rolls and the amount of funds spent on cash assistance have declined substantially since the creation of TANF. In 1994, the combined federal and state expenditures on AFDC cash assistance were $22.7 billion. By FY2011, this had declined to $9.6 billion. The decline would be even steeper in inflation-adjusted dollars.

In FY2011, TANF cash assistance was received by 1.9 million families per month. Within these families, there were 1.3 million work-eligible adults. The next several sections of this report

- provide a description of TANF work-eligible adults;
- briefly discuss TANF's work requirements as they apply directly to work-eligible individuals; and
- discuss the TANF work participation standards—the main performance measure for TANF that assesses state welfare-to-work efforts.

TANF WORK-ELIGIBLE INDIVIDUALS

Who Is a TANF Work-Eligible Individual?

Under TANF, work-eligible persons are either adult recipients of cash assistance or certain non-recipient parents of children receiving assistance who are expected to work. The following adults in TANF or MOE-funded households are *not* considered work-eligible:

- adult non-recipients who are non-parent caretakers (e.g., grandparent, aunt, uncle);
- ineligible noncitizen parents;
- at state option, adults receiving Supplemental Security Income (SSI);[46]

- parents who are needed in the home to care for disabled family members;
- at state option, parents who are Social Security Disability Insurance (SSDI) recipients; and
- at state option, a parent who became eligible for SSI during the fiscal year.

TANF Assistance Families with and without Work-Eligible Individuals

Figure 1 shows a breakdown of the types of families that received TANF assistance in FY2011. It shows that of all families receiving assistance, 61% included a work-eligible individual and 39% did not include a work-eligible individual in that year. Most TANF families with a work-eligible individual are single-parent families. In FY2011, single-parent families with a work-eligible individual comprised 55% of all TANF families; two-parent families with work-eligible individuals comprised 6% of all TANF families.

Characteristics of TANF Work-Eligible Individuals

TANF provides assistance to some of the most disadvantaged families with children. These are families that are not aided by the larger, more widely received social insurance programs such as Social Security Survivors, Social Security Disability, or Unemployment Insurance. The demographic characteristics of work-eligible individuals reflect those often associated with economic disadvantage. Most are single mothers, many with young children. Many of the mothers themselves are also young, either teen parents or young adults (under age 25) who might be considered "youths" in other contexts and programs.

TANF work-eligible individuals also tend to have lower educational attainment than the population as a whole, with 41% lacking a high school diploma or equivalent. Additionally, two-thirds of work-eligible individuals are minorities: African-Americans are 34.3% and Hispanics 25.9% of all TANF work-eligible individuals.

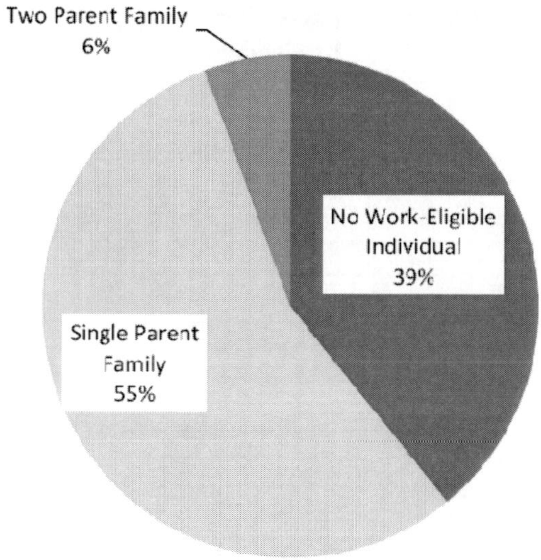

Source: Congressional Research Service tabulations of the FY2011 TANF National Data Files.

Notes: Information in this analysis differs slightly from the information HHS publishes with the official TANF work participation rates because of some differences in the data used to compute the work participation rates and the publically available TANF National Data Files. See Appendix B for a discussion of these differences.

Figure 1. TANF Assistance Families, by Family Type, FY2011.

Table 1 shows the summary characteristics of work-eligible individuals in FY2011. In that year, 84% of work-eligible individuals were women and 16% were men. Most of the women were not married, and 76% of them had never married. A little more than one-third of the women who were work-el i gi ble were under the age of 25. Men who were TA N F work-el igi ble were more likely to be married and living with a spouse (that is, i n two-parent families) and also tended to be slightly older.

A large share of TA N F work-eligible individuals had fai l ed to complete high school . For comparison with the general population, 37% of TA N F work-eligible women who were 25 and older did not complete high school, while 39% of TA N F work-eligible men did not complete high school . Among al l women age 25 and older i n 2011, 12% lacked a high school diploma or equivalent; among all men age 25 and older i n 2011, 13% lacked a high school diploma or equivalent.[47]

Table 1. Summary Characteristics of Work-Eligible Individuals: FY2011 By Gender

	Women	Men	Totals
Gender	84.4%	15.6%	100.0%
Marital Status			
Single never-married	75.8	48.5	71.5
Married living together	9.5	40.1	14.3
Married living apart	9.5	5.5	8.8
Widowed	0.3	0.8	0.4
Divorced	5.0	5.2	5.0
Totals	100.0	100.0	100.0
Age			
Teen parents	6.4	3.4	5.9
Age 20 to 24	28.6	14.2	26.3
Age 25 to 29	23.6	17.5	22.7
Age 30 to 34	17.3	18.4	17.5
Age 35 to 45	18.7	29.7	20.4
Age 45 and older	5.5	16.8	7.2
Total	100.0	100.0	100.0
Age of Youngest Child in Household			
Infant	18.7	16.6	18.3
1 to 3 years old	39.6	34.8	38.9
4 to 5 years old	13.2	12.2	13.0
6 to 12 years old	20.1	23.3	20.6
Age 13 and older	8.4	13.2	9.2
Total	100.0	100.0	100.0
Race/Ethnicity			
White, Non-Hispanic	31.8	41.4	33.3
Black, Non-Hispanic	36.8	20.5	34.3
Hispanic	25.7	27.1	25.9
American Indian or Alaskan Native	1.4	1.3	1.4
Asian or Pacific Islander	2.6	6.7	3.2
Unknown	1.7	3.0	1.9
Total	100.0	100.0	100.0
Educational Attainment			
Less than high school diploma	40.3	42.4	40.6
High school diploma or GED and above	57.8	55.0	57.4
Unknown	1.9	2.6	2.0
Total	100.0	100.0	100.0
Percent age 25 and above without a high school diploma or GED	37.0	39.0	37.4

Source: Congressional Research Service tabulations of the FY2011 TANF National Data files.

Notes: Information in this analysis differs slightly from the information HHS publishes with the official TANF work participation rates because of some differences in the data used to compute the work participation rates and the publically available TANF National Data Files. See Appendix B for a discussion of these differences.

The TANF national data files do not contain information necessary to examine the incidence of many "barriers" to employment. For example, they do not contain information on whether a work-eligible individual has a physical or mental impairment, substance abuse issues, or a criminal record.[48]

TANF's Work Requirements for Work-Eligible Individuals

All TANF's work requirements are actually requi rements on states as conditions of receiving federal block grant funds. There are essentially two sets of work requi rements: (1) those that requi re states to have certai n program rul es that apply di rectly to reci pi ents, which are descri bed i n the following sections; and (2) numerical performance standards computed i n the aggregate for each state. This second set of work requi rements is discussed later i n the report.

Federal Requirements That Apply to Individual Recipients

Federal TA N F law has three work-related requirements that states must apply to each adult or teen parent recipient: empl oyabi l i ty assessment, a requi rement that al l parents and caretakers be engaged i n work within 24 months, and sanctions for refusal to comply with work requi rements.

Employability Assessment

States are required to assess each adult recipient's or teen parent's skills, work experience, and employability. The assessment is required to be made within 90 days of determination of the recipient's eligibility for assistance. States may use this assessment to develop an Individual Responsi bi l i ty Plan (IRP) that sets forth employment goals and obligations of the recipient and describes the services the state will provide to the individual . The IRP is an option for the states; it is not requi red by federal law. States may sanction families for failure to comply with IRPs.[4]

Work within Two Years

States are required to engage each parent or caretaker adult in "work," as defined by the state, within 24 months of his or her coming on the rolls. For this requirement, the state is free to determine what constitutes being engaged in work; it need not follow the federal rules for the activities and hours that determine whether the family is counted as a participant toward the work participation performance standard (this standard is discussed later). This requirement is a part of the TANF state plan, and there is no specific penalty for a state that fails to engage a parent or caretaker in work by the 24-month deadline.

Sanctions for Failure to Comply with Work Requirements

States are required to sanction a family with a member who refuses to comply with its work requirements without "good cause." States are free to determine the sanction amount, and whether to reduce benefits or terminate benefits for families that fail to comply with work requirements (a full-family sanction). States also determine what constitutes good cause for not complying with work requirements. Under TANF, sanctions have become a more integral part of state programs and can sometimes result in the suspension or termination of the entire family grant.

States are prohibited from sanctioning a family with a single parent with a child under the age of six if he or she refuses to comply with work requirements because of an inability to find affordable child care. The parent must demonstrate to a state that the inability to find affordable child care is because (1) appropriate child care within a reasonable distance from the parent's work or home is unavailable, (2) informal child care by a relative or other arrangement is unavailable or unsuitable, and (3) appropriate and affordable child care is otherwise unavailable. The incidence of sanctioning in TANF assistance programs is discussed in the "Sanctions" section later in this report.

Activities of TANF Work-Eligible Individuals

What proportion of TANF work-eligible individuals are working or engaged in job preparation activities in a given month? **Figure 2** shows the work status of TANF work-eligible individuals in FY2011. It shows that on average in a month in FY2011,

- 42% of all TANF work-eligible individuals (about 548,000 persons) were reported as either employed or having participated for at least one hour in a job preparation activity during the month;

- participation in activities among TANF work-eligible individuals was split about evenly, with 21% of work-eligible individuals employed in unsubsidized jobs and 21% otherwise engaged in work or job preparation; and
- the majority (58%) of work-eligible individuals were reported as having no participation in the month.

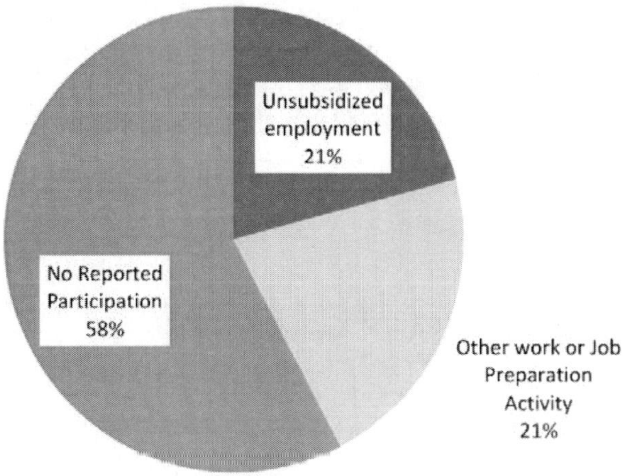

Source: Congressional Research Service tabulations of the FY2011 TANF National Data Files.

Notes: Information in this analysis differs slightly from the information HHS publishes with the official TANF work participation rates because of some differences in the data used to compute the work participation rates and the publically available TANF National Data Files. See Appendix B for a discussion of these differences.

Figure 2. Work Participation of TANF Work-Eligible Individuals: FY2011.

In FY2011, the overall rate of engagement was less than 50% in any given month. As discussed later, TANF requires states to ensure that a specified percentage of their caseload is participating in work requirements. The statute sets this percentage at 50% (90% for the two-parent portion of the caseload), but, as will be discussed in detail later, almost all states faced an effective participation standard below 50% in FY2011 because of credits against the standard. Thus, the lower rate of participation among work-related individuals does not mean that states, on average, failed their official work participation standards.

The overall rate of engagement discussed above is a monthly snapshot of work or participation in job preparation activities. Some recipients with no reported engagement may have been engaged in activities during earlier months; some may be engaged in later months. Engagement in work or job preparation activities measured over a period greater than one month (year, entire period a recipient received TANF) is likely to be higher than the monthly snapshot of engagement.[50] Some of the reasons that a work-eligible individual may have no reported participation include (1) being a newcomer to the rolls, with no activity yet assigned; (2) having completed an assigned activity and awaiting the beginning of a new activity; (3) the state has exempted the individual from work; (4) the state has determined that the work-eligible individual has good cause for failing to engage in work or activities; (5) the family is not complying with the state work requirement and is in the sanction process; or (6) the state has yet to engage the individual to participate.

Working While on the TANF Assistance Rolls

Of those participating in an activity, the most common activity of TANF work-eligible individuals has been working while still receiving assistance. States have adopted varying rules for treating families with a working adult. Some states disregard all earnings for a short period of time, allowing even those who get a full-time job to remain on the rolls for a transitional period. Other states disregard a portion of earnings indefinitely, providing an income supplement for low earners. Some states provide time-limited earnings supplements to families that have "left" the formal cash assistance program and have earnings.

Many states have more restrictive rules for those coming onto the rolls than for those who get a job while receiving assistance.[51] That is, their earnings cutoffs are lower for new applicants than for those on the rolls.

Participation of Work-Eligible Individuals by Selected Characteristics: FY2011

Table 2 examines participation in unsubsidized employment or other work or job preparation activity among TANF work-eligible individuals by selected characteristics in FY2011. It also shows participation separately for TANF work-eligible women and work-eligible men.

Participation in work activities varies little among men and women in total: an estimated 42.4% of work-eligible women and 41.9% of work-eligible men either were employed or participated in activities in FY2011. For both men and women, participation was lower for those without a high school diploma than for those with that credential. For TANF work-eligible women, participation rates in activities were lower for teen parents and for women aged 45 and older than for those between ages 20 and 44. Participation rates were also lower for women with infants than for those with older children, except that participation rates were also lower for women whose youngest child was a teen than for women whose youngest child was between the ages of 1 and 12. African-American women had a higher participation rate than women of other races and ethnicities.

In terms of participation among TANF work-eligible men, there was little variation in participation rates by the age of the youngest child in his family. Except for Asian and Pacific Islander men—who had a higher than average participation rate among TANF work-eligible men—there was little variation in participation rates by a man's race or ethnicity.

Table 2. TANF Work-Eligible Individuals Employed or Participating in a Work or Job Preparation Activity: by Characteristic, FY2011

	Unsubsidized Employment	Other Work or Job Preparation Activity	No Reported Participation	Total
Women	20.6%	21.8%	57.6%	100.0%
Men	22.1	19.8	58.1	100.0
Total	20.8	21.5	57.7	100.0
TANF Work-Eligible Women				
Marital Status				
Single never-married	20.2	22.2	57.6	100.0
Married living together	19.2	19.8	61.1	100.0
Married living apart	24.4	21.0	54.6	100.0
Widowed	13.7	31.6	54.7	100.0
Divorced	23.5	20.2	56.3	100.0
Total	20.6	21.8	57.6	100.0
Age				
Teen parents	13.5	24.2	62.4	100.0
Age 20 to 24	19.2	23.5	57.3	100.0
Age 25 to 29	23.3	21.1	55.6	100.0
Age 30 to 34	22.1	22.1	55.8	100.0
Age 35 to 45	20.7	20.3	59.0	100.0

Table 2. (Continued)

	Unsubsidized Employment	Other Work or Job Preparation Activity	No Reported Participation	Total
Age 45 and older	19.5	17.5	62.9	100.0
Total	20.6	21.8	57.6	100.0
Age of Youngest Child				
Infant	14.2	14.2	71.6	100.0
1 to 3 years old	22.3	25.6	52.1	100.0
4 to 5 years old	23.7	23.7	52.6	100.0
6 to 12 years old	22.9	22.4	54.8	100.0
Age 13 and older	19.2	17.4	63.4	100.0
Total	20.6	21.8	57.6	100.0
Race/Ethnicity				
White, Non-Hispanic	19.8	20.0	60.2	100.0
Black, Non-Hispanic	21.0	24.0	55.0	100.0
Hispanic	21.4	21.4	57.1	100.0
American Indian or Alaskan Native	18.0	21.9	60.1	100.0
Asian or Pacific Islander	17.9	16.4	65.7	100.0
Total	20.6	21.8	57.6	100.0
Educational Attainment				
Less than high school diploma	18.6	20.0	61.4	100.0
High school diploma or GED and above	22.3	23.6	54.1	100.0
Total	20.6	21.8	57.6	100.0
TANF Work-Eligible Men				
Marital Status				
Single never-married	18.8	18.9	62.4	100.0
Married living together	28.3	20.7	50.9	100.0
Married living apart	9.3	16.8	73.8	100.0
Widowed	24.9	39.7	35.3	100.0
Divorced	18.6	22.0	59.4	100.0
Total	22.1	19.8	58.1	100.0
Age				
Teen parents	11.2	11.9	76.8	100.0
Age 20 to 24	18.6	22.2	59.1	100.0
Age 25 to 29	22.7	19.6	57.7	100.0
Age 30 to 34	26.2	18.8	54.9	100.0
Age 35 to 45	21.8	20.5	57.7	100.0
Age 45 and older	22.6	19.5	57.8	100.0

	Unsubsidized Employment	Other Work or Job Preparation Activity	No Reported Participation	Total
Total	22.1	19.8	58.1	100.0
Age of Youngest Child				
Infant				
1 to 3 years old	22.4	20.0	57.6	100.0
4 to 5 years old	21.9	19.5	58.6	100.0
6 to 12 years old	26.2	23.3	50.5	100.0
Age 13 and older	21.2	20.0	58.8	100.0
Total	22.1	19.8	58.1	100.0
Race/Ethnicity				
White, Non-Hispanic	20.6	18.6	60.8	100.0
Black, Non-Hispanic	18.2	23.3	58.5	100.0
Hispanic	24.7	16.8	58.4	100.0
American Indian or Alaskan Native	13.2	23.0	63.9	100.0
Asian or Pacific Islander	32.9	24.7	42.4	100.0
Total	22.1	19.8	58.1	100.0
Educational Attainment				
Less than high school diploma	20.2	16.9	62.9	100.0
High school diploma or GED and above	23.9	22.8	53.3	100.0
Total	22.1	19.8	58.1	100.0

Source: Congressional Research Service tabulations of the FY2011 TANF National data files.

Notes: Information in this analysis differs slightly from the information HHS publishes with the official TANF work participation rates because of some differences in the data used to compute the work participation rates and the publically available TANF National Data Files. See Appendix B for a discussion of these differences.

Trends in Work Activity

Table 3 shows the percentage of TANF work-eligible persons either employed or otherwise engaged in work or job preparation in FY2011, and it compares these rates with selected prior years under TANF and one year under pre-TANF (FY1994) programs. As shown, reported participation under TANF has been considerably higher than under the pre-TANF programs, attributable in great part to the increase in regular unsubsidized employment among those on the rolls. The rate of participation in other activities also increased.

Within the TANF years shown (FY2000-FY2011), there has been little change in total participation. The rate at which recipients were employed in the earlier years of TANF (e.g., 2000) was greater than in the later years shown. This was partially offset by increases in the rate at which recipients were engaged in other activities.

Table 3. Percentage of Cash Assistance Adults and Teen Parents Employed or Engaged in a Work or Job Preparation Activity Selected Years FY1 994- FY2011

	1994	2000	2006	2011
Unsubsidized employment	8.3%	27.1%	22.0%	20.8%
Other work or job preparation activity	10.9	15.7	21.4	21.5
Total employed or in job preparation activity	19.2	42.8	43.4	42.3

Source: Congressional Research Service tabulations of the FY1994 Aid to Families with Dependent Children (AFDC) Quality Control data file and the FY2000, FY2006, and FY2011 TANF National Data files.

Notes: For FY1994 through FY2006, these figures represent the percentage of adult recipients; for FY201 1, they represent the percentage of TANF work-eligible individuals.

Sanctions

As discussed above, TANF law requires states to sanction families with a member who refuses to comply with work requirements, but it is the states that determine the actual sanction itself. Sanctions are not necessarily imposed for failure to meet the federal TANF work participation standards (e.g., hours requirements). They are imposed for failure to meet the requirements the state determines for an individual recipient.

Additionally, states have the flexibility to determine what may constitute "good cause" for not complying with work requirements. Though state definitions vary, a state may determine that a recipient has good cause for not participating because of a lack of transportation, domestic violence, lack of suitable employment, or illness.

Sanctions can range from partial reductions of the TANF grant to lifetime ineligibility. Over time, sanctions against work-eligible adults who do not meet the work requirements have become a significant component of many states' TANF programs.[52]

In recent years an increasing number of states have adopted policies to close cases (end benefits entirely) for families with members who do not comply with work requirements. In FY2001, eight jurisdictions ultimately closed cases when a family refused to comply with work requirements. By FY2011, this number had increased to 23 jurisdictions.

Table 4. TANF Families Sanctioned for Work, Educational, or Activity Requirements: FY2001-FY2011 Monthly Averages

	Families on the Rolls		Case Closures Due to Violating Work, Educational, or Activity Requirements		
Fiscal Year	Number of Sanctioned Families (thousands)	Percent of Total Families on the Rolls	Number of Families Sanctioned (thousands)	Percent of Total Families Leaving the Rolls	Combined Sanction Rate
2001	97.8	4.6%	10.8	6.5%	4.8
2002	109.2	5.3	10.1	6.0	5.4
2003	101.6	5.0	11.6	7.0	5.2
2004	81.9	4.1	16.4	9.7	4.6
2005	81.0	4.2	15.5	9.9	4.7
2006	70.6	3.9	13.4	8.8	4.3
2007	78.5	4.6	15.0	10.0	5.1
2008	70.2	4.3	16.0	11.2	4.9
2009	78.2	4.5	19.7	13.7	5.2
2010	72.9	3.9	21.5	14.0	4.7
2011	79.6	4.3	24.0	15.4	5.1

Source: Congressional Research Service tabulations of the FY2001-FY2011 TANF National Data Files.

Notes: Combined sanction rate represents the sum of families on the rolls with benefits reduced because of sanctions and families with cases closed because of failure to work or comply with an activity requirement divided by the sum of total families on the rolls and the total number of families leaving the rolls in a month.

The increasing number of states using case closure as the ultimate sanction is also reflected in data on TANF families on the rolls and those leaving the rolls. **Table 4** shows the number of sanctioned families, as well as the rate of sanctioning, for both those on the rolls as well as those leaving

TANF. In FY2001, a monthly average of about 98,000 families, or 4.6% of those on the rolls, was sanctioned for failing to comply with TANF work, educational, or activity requirements. In addition, during that year a monthly average of approximately 11,000 families, or 6.5% of all families leaving the rolls, had their cases closed because they failed to comply with a TANF work, education, or activity requirement. The overall sanction rate (combining those on the rolls and leavers) was 4.8%. Over time, the rate of sanctioning for those on the rolls has fluctuated some, but in FY2011 it was little changed from the rate observed in FY2001. However, both the absolute number as well as the percentage of those leaving the rolls because of a sanction has increased. In FY2011, 24,000 families were sanctioned off the rolls per month, representing 15.4% of all case closures.

The Claims Resolution Act of 2010, which extended TANF through the end of FY2011, required states to make supplementary reports on work participation and examine the circumstances of work-eligible individuals who are reported as having zero hours of participation in activities. In analyzing these data, HHS found that 16.7% of work-eligible individuals with zero reported hours of participation during the April-June 2011 quarter were either sanctioned or in the process of being sanctioned.[53]

The TANF Work Participation Standard: Measuring the Performance of State Welfare-to-Work Efforts

The previous section of this report describes how states have engaged work-eligible individuals in work or related activities. However, that is not how state welfare-to-work programs are formally assessed. This assessment is done through the TANF work participation standards, which is the focus of much of the attention on TANF's work provisions. These standards are set in federal law, and include target participation rates, rules for disregarding certain families from the participation rate, and rules for determining whether the state gets credit for participation in terms of countable activities and minimum hours requirements. States that fail to meet their target participation rates are at risk of being penalized through a reduction in their block grant.

The participation standard serves two purposes. First, it is a measure of how the state is performing in engaging recipients in work or work activities.

Secondly, it reinforces the notion that participation in work or work activities in return for receiving welfare assistance is a policy goal of TANF.

The purpose of this section is twofold:

1) it describes the detailed rules of the TANF work participation standard; and
2) it provides data (for FY2011) on the number of families included in the participation rate calculation, their engagement in countable work activities, and their hours of engagement.

TANF Work Participation: A Glossary of Terms

The language of TANF work requirements and work standards has its own nomenclature. Therefore, a review of the terms used, and their definitions, in discussions of TANF work requirements and standards might be helpful.

- Work-eligible individual. Generally parents (either recipients or non-recipients) and non-parent caretakers who themselves are recipients of TANF. Certain parents (discussed in detail above) are excluded from the definition of work-eligible individual. Non-recipient, non-parent caretakers are *not* considered work-eligible individuals.
- TANF work participation standard. The standard is the official assessment of state welfare-to-work programs under TANF law. It comprises: (1) a target rate of work participation; (2) a list of activities countable in the work participation rate; and (3) the minimum number of hours per week of participation in a month required for counting activities toward the work participation rate.
- Caseload Reduction Credit. A "credit" or reduction in the target rate of work participation granted for reducing the cash assistance rolls. States can also count as "caseload reduction," families aided by state spending in excess of what is required under the TANF MOE.
- Countable activities. A list of 12 activities (listed in law, defined in HHS regulations) that a work-eligible individual may engage in to have her or his participation counted toward the TANF work participation standards.

- Engaged in work. Represents the number of families participating in countable activities for at least the minimum number of hours.
- Family included in the TANF work participation rate. A family with at least one work-eligible individual and who is not disregarded from the participation rate.
- Work participation rate. A fraction (expressed as a percentage) derived by dividing the number of families considered "engaged in work" by the number of families included in the participation rate. It is the work participation rate that is compared to the target rate of work participation that determines whether a state has met the TANF work participation standard.

The Numerical Participation Standard

TANF sets minimum work participation standards that a state must meet. The standards are performance measures that apply in the aggregate for each state. They require that a specified percentage of families be considered engaged in specified activities for a minimum number of hours.

The TANF statute provides that 50% of all families and 90% of two-parent families must be engaged in work to meet the standard. However, few states have ever faced the full standard because the percentage is reduced for caseload reduction or state spending in excess of what is required under the TANF MOE. The caseload reduction credit reduces a state's 50% and 90% standards based on caseload reduction measured from FY2005. The caseload reduction credit reduces a state's numerical standards by one percentage point for each percent decline in the caseload. Additionally, under HHS regulations promulgated in 1999, states also may receive credits for spending in excess of what they are required to spend under the MOE requirement.[54] States may consider families assisted by excess MOE as "caseload reduction," and hence receive extra caseload reduction credits for such families.

For example, if a state achieves caseload reduction (including the effect of caseload reduction from excess MOE) of 25%, the state's work participation standard for the all-family standard is reduced by 25 percentage points—from 50% to 25%. If a state achieves caseload reduction of 50%, its all-family standard is reduced by 50 percentage points—from 50% to 0%.

Figure 3 portrays the effective (after-credit) participation standards for all families that states faced in FY2011. It categorizes the effective standards, which ranged from 0% (a state received a 50 percentage point or more caseload reduction credit) to 50% (state or territory had a 0 percentage point caseload reduction).

As the figure shows, 23 states faced effective all-family TANF work participation standards of 0% in FY2011. That is, they did not need to engage any families in activities to meet their standards. Two additional states faced effective standards from 1% to 9.9%; 8 states faced effective standards from 10% to 19.9%; 10 jurisdictions faced standards between 20% and 29.9%; six jurisdictions faced standards from 30% to 39.9%; three states faced standards from 40% to 49.9%; and two jurisdictions (South Dakota and Guam) faced the full 50% participation standard.

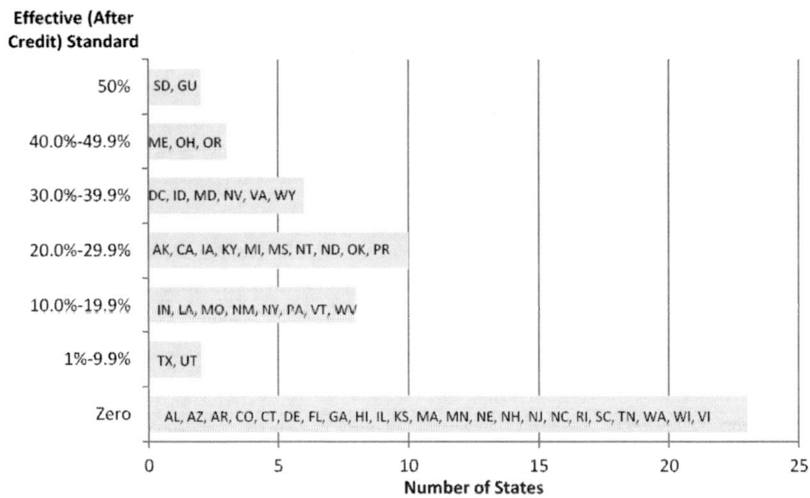

Source: Congressional Research Service, based on data from the U.S. Department of Health and Human Services (HHS).

Figure 3. TANF Effective (After-Credit) Work Participation Standards for FY2011.

Figure 10 will compare the TANF effective work participation standards with the work participation rates actually achieved.

The Work Participation Rate

A state's TANF work participation rate is computed and then compared to the state's effective (after-credit) standard. The work participation rate is a percentage, reflecting the number of families determined "engaged in work" divided by the total number of families included in the participation rate calculation. Not all families receiving cash assistance are included in the participation rate calculation, as some families do not have a "work-eligible" individual or are otherwise disregarded from the rate.

This section of this report describes in detail the rules for computing the TANF work participation rate. Along with the program rules, it displays FY2011 data indicating how many families were included in the rate calculation, as well as how families were engaged in activities in that year.

Families Included in the TANF Work Participation Rate

Only families receiving assistance from federal TANF or state MOE funds are included in the participation rate calculation. However, certain families receiving assistance are excluded either by statute or regulation. Such families may be exempted from TANF work requirements without creating the potential that their nonparticipation would result in a lower participation rate.

The families excluded from the participation rate are

- families without a work-eligible individual;
- at state option, families with a single parent caring for a child under the age of one—this exclusion is limited to a maximum of 12 months in a lifetime for the family;
- at state option, families participating in a tribal TANF or tribal work program; and
- families under a sanction for refusal to comply with work requirements, for up to three months in a 12-month period.

Figure 4 shows the percentage of families receiving TANF assistance that were included in the calculation of the work participation rate. As shown in the figure, after removing all families discussed above, a little more than half (54%) of all families receiving TANF assistance are included in the participation rate calculation. **Table 5** provides some more detail on families disregarded from the participation rate calculation. Most disregarded families were single-parent families with infants in FY2011. Such families accounted for 5.9% of all TANF assistance families and 80% of those families with a work-eligible individual but disregarded from the rate. The next largest category is families that are subject to sanction, at 1.5% of all TANF families. Though the percentage of TANF families disregarded because of participation in a tribal work program is small nationwide, it does comprise a fairly large share of the caseload in a few states (e.g., North Dakota).

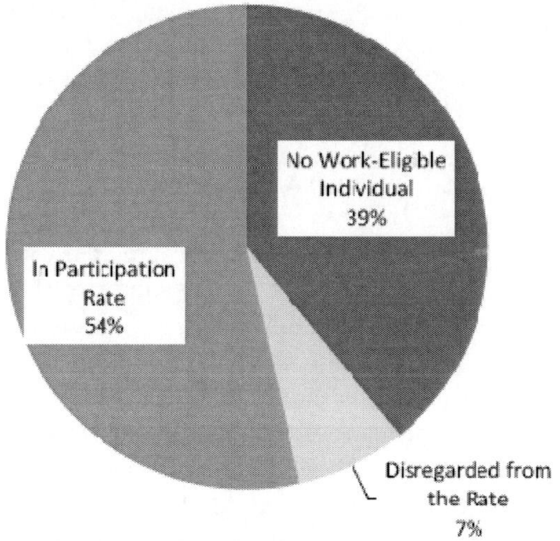

Source: Congressional Research Service tabulations of the FY2011 TANF National Data Files.

Notes: Information in this analysis differs slightly from the information HHS publishes with the official TANF work participation rates because of some differences in the data used to compute the work participation rates and the publically available TANF National Data Files. See Appendix B for a discussion of these differences.

Figure 4. TANF Assistance Families Included and Not Included in the Work Participation Rate: FY2011.

Table 5. TANF Assistance Families Included and Not Included in the TANF Work Participation Rate, FY2011

	Percent of Total TANF Families
Total TANF families	100.0%
No work-eligible individual	39.1
Disregarded from the participation rate calculation	7.4
Single parent with an infant	5.9
Sanctioned	1.5
Participating in tribal TANF or tribal work program	0.1
Included in the participation rate calculation	53.5

Source: Congressional Research Service tabulations of the FY2011 TANF National Data Files.

Notes: Information in this analysis differs slightly from the information HHS publishes with the official TANF work participation rates because of some differences in the data used to compute the work participation rates and the publically available TANF National Data Files. See Appendix B for a discussion of these differences.

Tribal TANF Programs

Individuals participating in a tribal TANF program can be excluded from the calculation of a state's work participation rate. Though CRS is not examining tribal TANF data in this report, a short discussion of tribal TANF as it pertains to work requirements may be informative.

Tribes, tribal organizations, and tribal consortia are authorized to receive and administer their own Tribal Family Assistance Grant for the support of activities that meet the same purposes as state TANF programs. However, tribes are not subject to all of the same work requirements that states are. Though there are hourly minimums and annual targeted participation rates that they must meet, each of these requirements is set by the tribe, in cooperation with the Department of Health and Human Services. At the recipient level, tribal TANF work activities are not subject to the same restrictions on vocational training as are placed on state TANF programs. Further, tribes may define their own individual work activities that count for the purposes of calculating their work participation rate, so recipients may have a different range of activities that may count towards their own hourly requirements.

Certain work requirements that tribes must meet are similar to the state requirements in some ways. For example, all work-eligible recipients are included in the calculation of the tribe's work participation rate, with a few exceptions. Parents with a child under one and parents subject to a sanction for less than three months in the last 12 months may be excluded from the tribe's work participation rate calculation. Further, like states, tribes may be subject to a sanction if they do not meet their work participation rate.

As discussed above, states determine what requirements apply to individual recipients. Thus, they have the option to *exempt* additional individuals and families from work requirements, which means that the family will not be sanctioned for failure to engage in work. However, such families will still be included in the calculation of the work participation rate.

Engaged in Work: Countable Activities

Work-eligible individuals must participate in specific activities during a month to be considered "engaged in work" and count toward the work participation standard. Work-eligible individuals must also participate in activities for a minimum number of hours per week in a month to be considered "engaged in work."

Federal law lists 12 categories of activities creditable toward meeting TANF work participation standards. HHS regulations define what specific types of activities count under each of the 12 categories. **Table 6** lists the 12 creditable categories of activities and the HHS regulatory definition for each. As shown in the table, the specific activities included in the 12 categories are fairly comprehensive in terms of welfare-to-work activities, and include education (including attendance at four-year colleges) as well as rehabilitative activities. However, as will be discussed below, the "pre-employment" activities of job search, rehabilitation, and education are limited in terms of how long or under what circumstances they can be counted toward the official participation standard.

Table 6. Countable TANF Work Activities and Their Definitions

Activity	Definition
Unsubsidized employment	Full-or part-time employment in the public or private sector that is not subsidized by TANF or any other public program.
Subsidized private sector employment	Employment in the private sector for which the employer receives a subsidy from TANF or other public funds to offset some or all of the wages and costs of employing an individual.
Subsidized public sector employment	Employment in the public sector for which the employer receives a subsidy fromTANF or other public funds to offset some or all of the wages and costs of employing an individual.
Job search and readiness Participation in this activity may be countedfor six weeks (12 weeks in certain circumstances) in a fiscal year.	The act of seeking or obtaining employment, or preparation to seek or obtain employment, including life-skills training and substance abuse treatment, mental health treatment, or rehabilitation activities. Such treatment or therapy must be determined to be necessary and documented by a qualified medical, substance abuse, or mental health professional.

Table 6. (Continued)

Activity	Definition
Community service	Structured programs and embedded activities in which TANF recipients performwork for the direct benefit of the community under the auspices of public or nonprofit organizations. Community service programs must be limited to projects that serve a useful community purpose in fields such as health, social service, environmental protection, education, urban and rural redevelopment, welfare, recreation, public facilities, public safety, and child care. A state agency shall take into account, to the extent possible, the prior training, experience, andskills of an individual inmaking appropriate community service assignments.
Work experience	Awork activity, performed in return for welfare, that provides an individual withan opportunity to acquire the general skills, knowledge, and work habits necessary to obtain employment.The purpose of work experience is to improvethe employability of an individual who cannot find unsubsidized full-time employment.
On-the-job training	Training in the public or private sector that is given to a paid employee while he or she is engaged in productive work and that provides knowledge and skills essential to the full and adequate performance of the job.
Vocational educational training	Organized educational programs that are directly related to the preparation of individuals for employment in current or emerging occupations.
Participation in this activity is limited to 12 months in a lifetime.	
Caring for a child of a recipient in community service	Providing child care to enable another cash welfare recipient to participate in a communityservices program. This is an unpaid activity and must be a structured program to improve the employability of participating individuals.
Job skills training directly related to employment	Training or education for job skills required by an employer to provide an individual with the ability to obtain employment or to advance or adapt to the changing demands of the workplace.
Education directly related to employment (for those without a high school or equivalent degree)	Education related to a specific occupation, job, or job offer.

Activity	Definition
Completion of a secondary school program (for those without a high school or equivalent degree)	In the case of a recipient who has not completed secondary school or received such a certificate, this means regular attendance, in accordance with the requirements of a secondary school or course of study, at a secondary school orin a course of study leading to a certificate of general equivalence.

Source: Table prepared by CRS based on HHS regulations. See *Federal Register*, vol. 73, no. 24, February 5, 2008, pp. 6772-6828.

Figure 5 shows the percentage of work-eligible individuals in families included in the participation rate by their activity. The percentage of such individuals participating at least one hour in a month in each of the 12 countable activities is presented. As evidenced in the figure, unsubsidized employment—work in a regular job while receiving cash assistance—was by far the most common work activity in FY2011 with 22.8% of work-eligible individuals included in the participation rate in that activity. The time-limited pre-employment activities of job search and readiness (10.7% of all individuals in families included in the participation rate) and vocational educational training (5.9% of such individuals) were the next most common activities.

Unsubsidized Employment

As discussed earlier, the most common activity of TANF work-eligible individuals in families included in the participation rate was unsubsidized employment: working in a regular job while on the rolls during a month.

States get credit toward their work participation standard for working families on assistance. This encourages them to disregard earnings, providing an earnings supplement for at least a limited period of time. As discussed in the section on welfare-to-work research, evaluated programs with earnings supplements tended to increase work and also raised the incomes of families in those programs.

Though a higher proportion of TANF families have earnings than families who received benefits in the pre-1996 program, the smaller caseload means that TANF earnings supplements reach fewer families than occurred before welfare reform. However, the more widely received Earned Income Tax Credit (EITC); Additional Child Tax Credit (ACTC); and other need-tested programs, such as the Supplemental Nutrition Assistance Program (SNAP), also aid low-income working families with children and thus supplement their earnings.

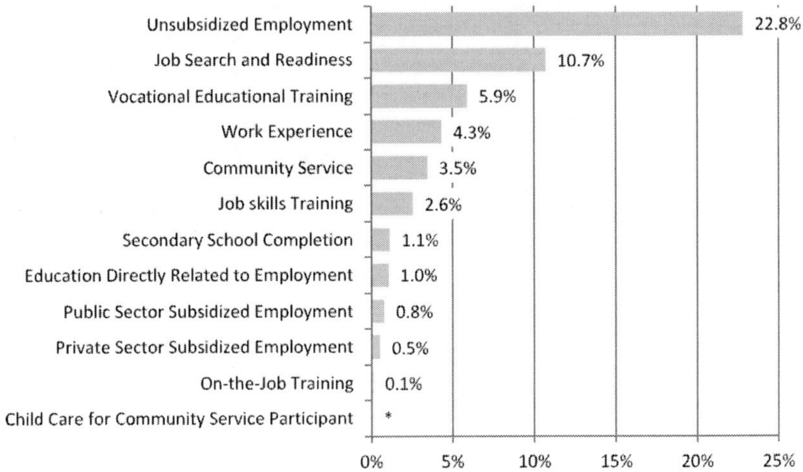

Source: Congressional Research Service tabulations of the FY2011 TANF National Data Files.

Notes: * Indicates less than 0.05%. Information in this analysis differs slightly from the information HHS publishes with the official TANF work participation rates because of some differences in the data used to compute the work participation rates and the publically available TANF National Data Files. See Appendix B for a discussion of these differences.

Figure 5. Percentage of TANF Work-Eligible Individuals Included in the Participation Rate in TANF Work Activities: FY2011. (Excludes Work-Eligible Individuals Disregarded from the TANF Work Participation Rate Calculation).

Subsidized Employment

In FY2011, the rate at which TANF work-eligible individuals included in the participation rate were engaged in subsidized employment was low: 0.5% reported engagement during a month in subsidized *private* sector employment and 0.8% reported engagement during a month in subsidized *public* sector employment. Subsidized employment has historically been relatively rare in TANF welfare-to-work programs.

However, the American Recovery and Reinvestment Act of 2009 (ARRA, P.L. 111-5) established a two-year Emergency Contingency Fund that provided states with extra federal dollars that could help finance increased expenditures on subsidized employment in FY2009 and FY2010. The ARRA fund did help finance subsidized employment, but most of this activity occurred in FY2010. It is unknown the degree to which the ARRA funds were used to finance subsidized employment for those on the assistance rolls versus those who were not receiving TANF assistance. Only in the former case (for those on the assistance rolls) would subsidized employment be present in the work participation data. States receive no credit toward their TANF work standards for subsidized employment for those who are not on the benefit rolls.

Time-Limited Job Search and Readiness and Vocational Educational Training

The two most common activities that TANF work-eligible individuals engage in other than unsubsidized employment are job search and readiness and vocational educational training. In FY2011, 10.7% of TANF work-eligible individuals included in the participation rate calculation were in job search and readiness. That year, 5.9% of such persons were engaged in vocational educational training.

These two activities are countable only for a specified period of time. The combination of job search and job readiness activities counts for only a maximum of 12 weeks in a fiscal year. HHS regulations afford states some flexibility by setting the weekly limit in hourly equivalents, allowing job search and readiness to be counted in more than 12 calendar weeks in a year.

Vocational educational training can only be counted for 12 months in a recipient's lifetime. Additionally, the combination of vocational educational training and teen parents determined engaged in work by virtue of education cannot exceed 30% of all families determined engaged in work. Participation in such activities over that limit does not count toward the TANF work participation rate.

"Workfare"

Work experience is the fourth most common activity of TANF work-eligible individuals included in the participation rate, with 4.3% of such individuals engaged in that activity in FY2011. An additional 3.5% of TANF work-eligible individuals included in the participation rate were engaged in community service in that year.

Work experience and community service are two activities typically thought of as "workfare": performing a form of work in return for their cash assistance benefits. Such activities could also be viewed as helping individuals obtain certain skills, such as developing work habits and other job skills. Most states have not adopted large-scale workfare programs under TANF, but these two activities are relatively prevalent in some states.

On-the-Job Training

States may count most education and training activities in only a limited way toward the TANF work participation standards. The exception is on-the-job training: training provided to a participant in a paid job. States can count hours spent in this activity under any circumstance. However, engagement in on-the-job training is relatively rare. In FY2011, 0.1% of all TANF work-eligible adults included in the participation rate were participating in on-the-job training.

Education

For adult recipients (defined in TANF as age 20 and older), engagement in educational activities such as secondary school completion, education directly related to employment, and job skill training count only under limited circumstances or in combination with other activities. Combining work and education will be discussed in a separate section of this report, below.

Engaged in Work: Hours of Participation

To be considered a "participant" and counted by a state toward meeting its standard, a family member or members must also be engaged in these activities for a minimum number of hours per week in a month. The required minimum hours per week in a month vary by the family's composition.

Table 7 outlines the TANF work participation hours standards. For meeting the "all family" standard, the hours requirement varies depending on family type and the age of the youngest child. The general hours requirement is an average of at least 30 hours per week during the month. However, for single parents caring for a child under the age of six, an average of 20 hours per week during the month is needed in work activities for a state to deem them participants. More hours are required for two-parent families to meet the standard. In two-parent families, the combined hours of both parents are considered in determining whether a family can be considered a participant family.

Table 7 shows that certain hours of participation must be in "core" activities, while remaining hours may be in "supplemental" activities. The concepts of core and supplemental activities are discussed later in this report.

Table 7. TANF Hours Requirements for the All-Family Rate and the Two-Parent Family Rate (Excludes Special Rule for Teen Parents), by Family Type

	All-Family Rate			**Two-Parent Family Rate(Parents may combine hours)**
Single-Parent Families with a Child Under Age 6	**Other Families**	**Two-Parent Families Receiving Federally Funded Child Care**		**Two-Parent Families not Receiving Federally Funded Child Care**
Total hours requirement	An average of 20 hours per week during the month	An average of 30 hours per week during the month	An average of 55 hours per week during the month	An average of 35 hoursper week during the month
Required hours incore activities the month	An average of 20 hours per week during during the month	An average of 20 hours per week during the month	An average of 50 hours per week during the month	An average of 30 hoursper week during the month
Allowable hours insupplemental activities	Not applicable	Up to an average of 10 hours per week during the month	Up to an average of 5 hours per week during the month	Up to an average of 5 hours per week duringthe month

Source: Table prepared by CRS.

HHS regulations clarify that only actual hours of participation count toward meeting these standards. However, they also created an excused absence policy. For paid activities, states are credited for all hours for which an individual is paid, including any holidays or paid leave (e.g., paid sick leave). For unpaid activities, the regulations allow for up to 10 holidays plus 80 hours of other excused absences over a year.

The regulations require that hours in unpaid activities be supervised on a daily basis. The daily supervision requirement means that a responsible party has daily oversight of an individual's participation, not necessarily daily in-person contact with the participant.

Figure 6 shows a breakdown of the families that were included in the work participation rate in FY2011 (e.g., families with a work-eligible individual that were not disregarded). Families are classified based on their statutory hours requirements:

- teen parents without a high school diploma, who may be deemed engaged in work through completion of secondary school or 20 hours of education directly related to employment;
- single parents with a child under the age of 6, who may be deemed engaged in work through 20 hours of participation in countable activities;
- single parents with all children aged 6 or older, who are required to participate in activities for 30 hours per week; and
- two-parent families.[55]

In FY2011, the largest category of families included in the participation rate was single parents with a pre-school aged child (under the age of 6). This group represented close to half (48.7%) of all TANF families included in the participation rate. The second largest group in FY2011 was single parents with all children aged 6 and older, representing 38.0% of all TANF families included in the participation rate. In FY2011, two-parent families represented 10.4% of all TANF families included in the participation rate, most of whom did not report receipt of federally funded child care. In FY2011, only 0.2% of all families included in the participation rate were two-parent families that received federally funded child care. This category is not shown separately on the figure. Teen parents without a high school diploma represented 2.9% of all FY2011 TANF families included in the participation rate.

Special Rule for Teen Parents Who Lack High School Diplomas

Teen parents who are included in the TANF work participation rate calculation have a special rule for determining whether they are engaged in work. A state may deem a teen parent who lacks a high school diploma as engaged in work if she or he is participating in education directly related to employment for an average of at least 20 hours per week during the month or is making satisfactory progress toward completion of a secondary school program, including a program leading to a General Educational Development diploma. However, such participation of a teen parent may not count toward the participation standard if a state exceeds a cap on participation in education. The education cap is that no more than 30% of those considered engaged in work may be considered engaged through the combination of vocational educational training or teen parents deemed "engaged in work" through education.

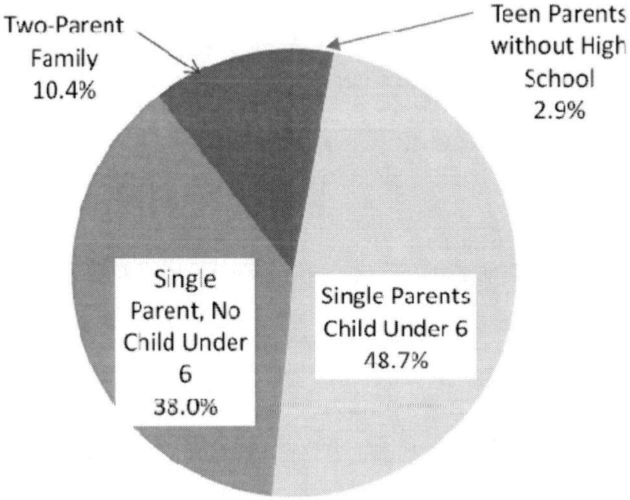

Source: Congressional Research Service tabulations of the FY2011 TANF National Data Files.

Notes: Information in this analysis differs slightly from the information HHS publishes with the official TANF work participation rates because of some differences in the data used to compute the work participation rates and the publically available TANF National Data Files. See Appendix B for a discussion of these differences.

Figure 6. TANF Families Included in the Work Participation Rate, By Family Type, FY2011. (Excludes Families with Work-Eligible Individuals Disregarded from the TANF Work Participation Rate Calculation).

Table 8 shows the work or job preparation engagement of teen parents included in the participation rate. (For minor teens, under the age of 18, only teens that are heads of households or married to heads of households are included in the participation rate. TANF minor teen parents living in other settings—such as unmarried teens living with their parents or in an alternative adult-supervised setting—are excluded from the participation rate calculation.)

Of such work-eligible persons, 15.4% were deemed engaged in work through education—completing high school, in a GED program, or participating at least 20 hours in education directly related to employment. The percent of teen parents without a high school diploma deemed engaged in work through education declined from 33.3% for those aged 17 to 20.6% for those aged 18, and further declined to less than 10% for those aged 19. This reflects a low rate of take-up on the option states have to engage and count teens aged 18 and 19 through GED programs.

Table 8. TANF Work Participation Among Teen Parents Included in the Participation Rate Without a High School Diploma, by Age, FY2011
(Excludes Teen Parents Who Are Not Work-Eligible Individuals or Who Are Work Eligible Individuals But Disregarded from the TANF Work Participation Rate Calculation)

	Deemed Engaged Through Education	Employed	Participating in Other Activities	Total Participating
Under age 17	25.7%	4.6%	4.1%	34.3%
Age 17	33.3	2.4	5.1	40.8
Age 18	20.6	6.4	6.8	33.8
Age 19	9.9	17.0	11.9	38.8
Totals	15.4	12.0	9.5	36.8

Source: Congressional Research Service tabulations of the FY2011 TANF National Data Files.

Note: Information in this analysis differs slightly from the information HHS publishes with the official TANF work participation rates because of some differences in the data used to compute the work participation rates and the publically available TANF National Data Files. See Appendix B for a discussion of these differences.

Hours of Participation of Single-Parent Families

There are some differences in the number of hours of participation for single parents based on whether they have a child under age 6 or not. **Figure 7** shows the distribution of families by hours of participation among single-parent families included in the participation rate, by family category in FY2011. Two major differences in the categories are apparent in the figure. First, single-parent families with children under age 6 are more likely to have some hours of participation than are single-parent families with older children who are included in the participation rate. There was a 7% gap for families with zero hours—58.7% for families included in the participation rate with a child aged 6 and older versus 52.0% for families included in the participation rate with a pre-school-aged child. Note that excluded from families with a pre-school-aged child are those single parents with an infant who the state has opted to exclude from the participation rate.

The second difference shown in the figure represents hours of participation over 20 hours per week. It shows that the different hours requirements might have had some impact on actual hours of participation. The share of single parents with a child under 6—subject to a 20-hour per week requirement—exceeded the share of single parents with an older child participating 20 hours per week or 21 to 29 hours per week. The share of single parents with no child under age 6—subject to a 30-hour per week requirement—exceeded the share of single parents with a child under age 6 participating 30 hours or more per week.

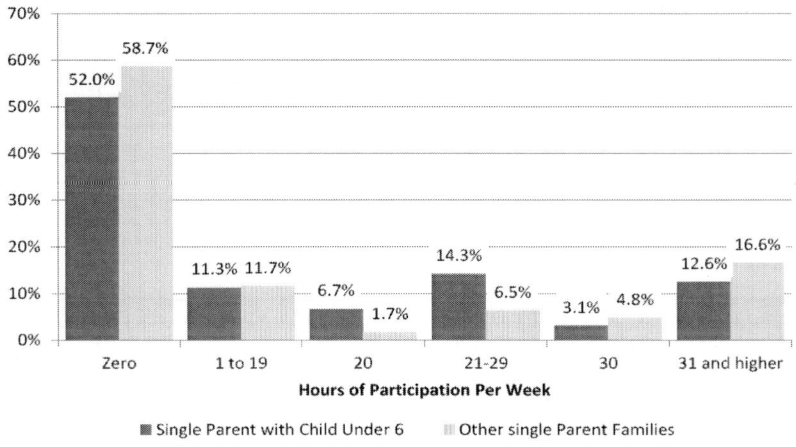

Source: Congressional Research Service tabulations of the FY2011 TANF National Data Files.

Notes: Information in this analysis differs slightly from the information HHS publishes with the official TANF work participation rates because of some differences in the data used to compute the work participation rates and the publically available TANF National Data Files. See Appendix B for a discussion of these differences.

Figure 7. Distribution of TANF Single Parent Families Included in the TANF Work Participation Rate by Hours of Participation in Activities and by Presence of a Child Under Age 6 in the Family, FY2011. (Excludes Families with Work-Eligible Individuals Disregarded from the TANF Participation Rate Calculation).

Hours of Participation of Two-Parent Families

Figure 8 shows the distribution of TANF two-parent families included in the participation rate calculation by hours of participation in FY2011.[56] The figure shows that only 37.7% of two-parent families had zero hours of participation. Thus, two-parent families were more likely to have some reported hours of participation than were single-parent families. However, they were also more likely to fall short of their hours requirement. About 30% of two-parent families had between one hour and 34 hours of participation per week during the month. Most two-parent families are subject to a 35-hour requirement. In contrast, among single-parent families with a child under the age of six included in the participation rate, 11% had hours between one and their 20-hour per week standard. Among other single-parent families, about 20% had hours between one and their 30-hour per week standard. (See Table 7 for a summary of the hours requirements.)

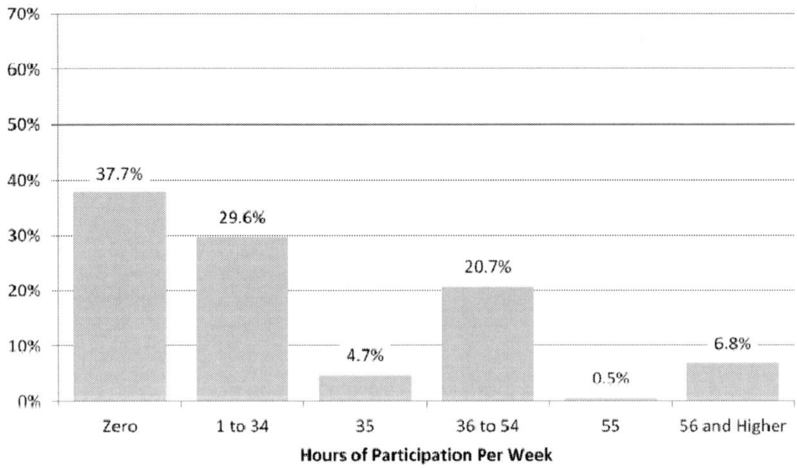

Source: Congressional Research Service tabulations of the FY2011 TANF National Data Files.

Notes: Information in this analysis differs slightly from the information HHS publishes with the official TANF work participation rates because of some differences in the data used to compute the work participation rates and the publically available TANF National Data Files. See Appendix B for a discussion of these differences.

Figure 8. Distribution of TANF Two-Parent Families Included in the TANF Work Participation Rate by Hours of Participation in Activities, FY2011. (Excludes Families with Work-Eligible Individuals in Families Disregarded from the TANF Work Participation Rate).

Combining Education and Work

In general, TANF work rules emphasize that adult recipients (defined as age 20 and older) should be in activities that emphasize quick attachment to the labor force. However, these rules also allow states to get credit for recipients who combine work with education.

Table 9 lists the 12 activities (described in **Table 6**), classifying them as either "core" or "supplemental." In general, participation in a core activity may be a recipient's sole or primary activity used to fully satisfy TANF participation requirements. On the other hand, participation in supplemental activities often must be done only in conjunction with participation in core activities, with hours that count only after the core requi rement is met.

M ost of the core activities focus on work or activities designed to move a family quickly i nto work. The notable exception is vocational educational training, which is creditable for 12 months i n an individual's lifetime as a sole or primary TANF activity. All supplemental activities are education-related.

Table 9. TANF "Core" and "Supplemental" Work Activities

"Core" activities	• Unsubsidized employment • Subsidized private sector employment • Subsidized public sector employment • Job search and readiness (Usual limit of six weeks in a fiscal year.This limit is converted to an "hourly equivalent" basis, see below)a • Community service • Work experience • On-the-job training • Vocational educational training (limited to 12 months in an individual's lifetime) • Caring for a child of a recipient in community service.
"Supplemental" activities	• Job skills training directly related to employment • Education directly related to employment (for those without a high school or equivalent degree) • Completion of a secondary school program (for those without a high school orequivalent degree)

Source: Table prepared by CRS.

a. The limit on job search and readiness is increased to 12 weeks for a state that has an unemployment rate at least 50% above the national average unemployment rate or that meets the "economic need" criteria for TANF contingency funds.

Figure 9 shows that the combination of work and education is relatively rare for TANF work-eligible persons. In FY2011, only 4.5% of the individuals included in the participation rate participated in both education and work-related activities. "Education activities" refer to hours spent in vocational education training, job skills training directly related to employment, work experience (i.e., education directly related to employment for an individual without a high school diploma or GED), and satisfactory school attendance for individuals without a high school diploma or GED. Education-related activities are intended to provide recipients with a greater opportunity for career advancement; however, there are limitations on the level of participation in those activities that are countable toward a state's work participation rate.

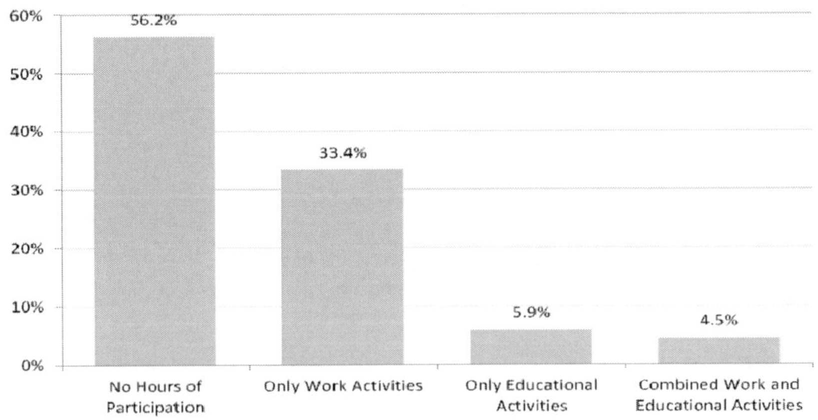

Source: Congressional Research Service tabulations of the FY2011 TANF National Data Files.

Notes: The number of families with no hours of participation in this figure differs from that reported in Figure 2 and Table 2 because work-eligible individuals in families disregarded from the participation rate are excluded from the analysis in this figure. Information in this analysis differs slightly from the information HHS publishes with the official TANF work participation rates because of some differences in the data used to compute the work participation rates and the publically available TANF National Data Files. See Appendix B for a discussion of these differences.

Figure 9. Percentage of TANF Work-Eligible Individuals Included in the Work Participation Rate Who Participated in Work- and Education-Related Activities, FY2011. (Excludes Individuals in Families Disregarded from the TANF Work Participation Rate Calculation).

FY2011 Participation Rates

The percent of families included in the TANF work participation calculation who are in creditable activities for at least the minimum required hours is the official TANF work participation rate. For FY2011, the national average work participation rate was 29.5% for all families. Under TANF, each jurisdiction's annual work participation rate is computed and compared with its effective (after-credit) standard. **Figure 10** shows each jurisdiction's FY2011 all-family participation rate and compares it to the effective (after-credit) standard for that state for all families.

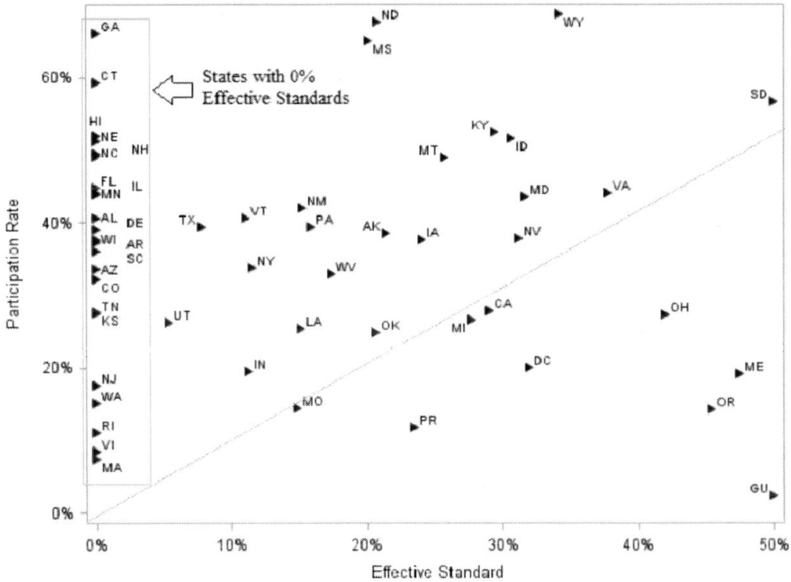

Source: Source: Congressional Research Service, based on data from the U.S. Department of Health and Human Services (HHS).

Notes: For a tabular presentation of FY2011 TANF effective standards and participation rates, see Table A-4.

Figure 10. TANF Effective Work Participation Standards and Work Participation Rates, by State, FY2011.

The 45-degree line on the figure shows where a jurisdiction's participation rate would equal its standard. Thus, those jurisdictions shown above the 45-degree line met (or more than met) their standards; those below the 45-degree line failed to meet their standard. The figure shows that nine jurisdictions failed to meet their all-family work standards in FY2011: California, Guam, the District of Columbia, Maine, Michigan, Missouri, Ohio, Oregon, and Puerto Rico. It also shows that there is no apparent relationship between a state's effective standard and its actual participation rate. States with a 0% effective (after-credit) standard had participation rates that ranged from 7.3% in Massachusetts to 66.0% in Georgia. Jurisdictions that failed to meet the participation standard had rates that ranged from 2.3% in Guam to 27.8% in California.

Trends in "Effective" Work Standards and Rates, FY2002-FY2011

States first faced the 50% statutory work participation standard in FY2002. The 1996 welfare law gradually increased the statutory standards from 25% in FY1997 to 50% in FY2002. FY2011 was typical in terms of the history of TANF's work participation rate. States have generally faced effective standards far lower than 50%; the work participation rate has hovered in the neighborhood of 30% since FY2002.

Trends in Effective Standards

A state's effective TANF all-family work participation standard is its statutory standard (50%) minus credits it receives for caseload reduction and for state spending beyond that required by the TANF maintenance of effort requirement. **Table 10** shows the number of jurisdictions with effective participation standards of 0%; from 1% to 9.9%; from 10% to 24.9%; from 25% to 49.9%; and 50% for FY2002 through FY2011. In FY2008 through FY2010, 22 jurisdictions faced a 0% work participation standard. In FY2011, 23 jurisdictions faced a 0% effective (after credit) work standard. In FY2011, only Guam and South Dakota faced the full 50% standard.

Before FY2007, caseload reduction was measured from FY1995. The Deficit Reduction Act of 2005 (P.L. 109-171) made the change in the credit, measuring caseload reduction from FY2005. Before FY2006, most of the reduction of the work participation standard came from caseload reduction. Nationally, caseloads declined by 57% from FY1995 through FY2005. Caseload reduction credits were much reduced in FY2007, when credits were based on caseload change only from FY2005 to FY2006. In that year, four jurisdictions faced a zero participation standard. However, beginning in FY2008 states began to rely on the "excess MOE" portion of the caseload reduction credit, and effective standards again were substantially reduced. The Government Accountability Office (GAO) found that in FY2009, 16 states would not have met their TANF work participation standards had they not claimed excess MOE credits.[57]

Table 10. Effective TANF Work Participation Standards for All Families: FY2002-FY2011 Number of Jurisdictions by Category of Effective Work Participation Standards

	Pre-DRA Caseload Reduction Credit						Post-DRA Caseload Reduction Credit			
	2002	2003	2004	2005	2006	2007	2008	2009	2010	2011
Zero	21	20	18	17	19	4	22	22	22	23
0%-9.9%	21	15	17	16	14	5	0	1	3	2
10.0%-19.9%	7	11	11	14	14	6	10	10	8	8
20.0%-29.9%	3	6	3	4	4	10	8	9	11	10
30.0%-39.9%	1	0	4	2	2	15	7	7	5	6
40.0%-49.9%	0	1	0	0	0	12	4	3	3	3
50%	1	1	1	1	1	2	3	2	2	2

Source: Congressional Research Service tabulations of data from the U.S. Department of Health and Human Services.

Notes: DRA is the Deficit Reduction Act of 2005 (P.L. 109-171). Before the effective year of the DRA (2007), the caseload reduction credit measured caseload change from FY1995. For FY2007 and thereafter (post –DRA caseload reduction credit), the caseload reduction credit measured caseload change from FY2005.

The American Recovery and Reinvestment Act of 2009 (ARRA, P.L. 111-5) allowed states that experienced caseload increases during the recent recession to freeze their caseload reduction credits at pre-recession levels. This freeze applied only to reductions in work participation standards through FY2011. Beginning in FY2012, this freeze expires and states will receive credit for caseload change from FY2005 to FY2011. Additionally, HHS regulations that standardized the calculation of the excess MOE portion also take effect in FY2012.[58] These two changes would reduce credits—and potentially raise effective (after-credit) participation standards—for states that either had caseload increases because of the recession or used more liberal methodologies in computing the "excess MOE" portion of the caseload reduction credit.

Trends in Work Participation Rates

Figure 11 shows the national average TANF work participation rate for all families based on the federal rules for FY2002 through FY2011. The rate shown in the figure excludes the effect of grandfathered, pre-1996 welfare law waivers. (See text box below for a discussion of the "grandfathered" waivers.)

In FY2011, the national average TANF work participation rate was 29.5%. The figure shows that the participation rate has fluctuated around 30% since FY2002, remaining well below 50% for the entire period. However, as noted previously, most states met their participation standards with rates below 50% because of caseload reduction and excess MOE credits.

Grandfathered" AFDC Waivers Under TANF

After the enactment of the welfare reform law of 1996, states created TANF programs that required work, and provided financial incentives and earnings supplements to families that moved into the workforce. Many states that tested new programs under "waivers" of pre-1996 law used them as the basis for their TANF programs. TANF allowed states to continue their waiver programs even if they were inconsistent with TANF rules until the expiration of those waiver programs. States that continued their work-related waivers were permitted to have their programs assessed based on the rules of their waivers rather than those of the federal work participation standard.[59] In general, states that operated under waivers still had to achieve the numerical participation standards required under the new law. However, they were able to count certain participation that otherwise would not meet the federal definition of "engaged in work." This included activities not countable toward the participation standard, such as extended job search and education. It also included families participating for fewer hours than required under that federal definition. Further, states were also permitted to exclude from the participation-rate calculation families that were exempted from the welfare-to-work program under their waiver. A total of 20 states continued their waiver programs under TANF. The last of these programs (Tennessee's) expired in 2007. In FY2011, all state welfare-to-work programs were assessed using the federal TANF work participation standards.

A Note on the Two-Parent Family Standard

Historically, most families receiving cash assistance have been single-parent families, usually headed by a single mother. However, some two-parent families receive assistance. Under TANF's work participation standards, these families are subject to a higher standard: 90% of these families must be engaged in work, though the two-parent standard can also be reduced for caseload reduction. Additionally, more hours of participation are required of two-parent families. The work-eligible adults in two-parent families must participate in activities for at least 35 hours per week in a month; if the family receives federally funded child care, at least 55 hours per week in a month are required (the hours requirement applies to the total hours of engagement by both parents).

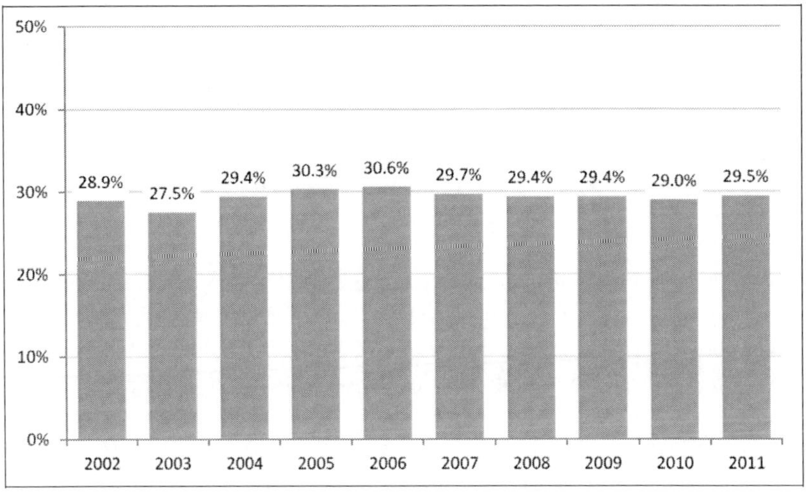

Source: Congressional Research Service, based on data from the U.S. Department of Health and Human Services.

Figure 11. National Average TANF Work Participation Rate for All Families, FY2002-FY2011. Based on Federal Rules; Does not Include the Effects of Pre-1996 Work Waivers in FY2002-FY2007.

Many states have avoided the need to meet the two-parent family standard. Before FY2007, many states aided two-parent families in "separate state programs." Separate state programs are state programs with expenditures counted toward the TANF MOE but not considered TANF programs. Before FY2007, cash assistance families in separate state programs were not included in the work participation rate and thus not subject to TANF's work participation standards. The Deficit Reduction Act of 2005 (P.L. 109-171) brought families in separate state programs into the calculation of TANF participation rates, thus subjecting them to the standards effective in FY2007. However, many states then moved these families to "solely state funded programs," with expenditures that are not countable toward TANF's MOE and thus totally outside of TANF's rules, including work participation. In FY2011, 27 jurisdictions had two-parent families included in their TANF or MOE caseloads. Of these, five failed to meet their two-parent work participation standard (Maine, Nevada, Oregon, Rhode Island, and Guam).

Implications for Failing the Standard

States that fail the TANF work participation standards are at risk of a financial penalty in the form of a reduced block grant. The TANF statute penalizes a state 5% of its block grant for the first year in which it fails to meet the standards, with the penalty increasing two percentage points for each subsequent year's failure, to a maximum of 21% of the block grant.

However:

- The statute provides that the Secretary of HHS may reduce the penalty based on the severity of the failure. HHS regulations specify a formula for reducing the penalty based on (1) the gap between a state's participation rate and its after-credit standard, (2) any increase in the number of families engaged in work from the preceding fiscal year, and (3) the number of years the state has failed the standard. A state that fails only the two-parent standard will have its penalty reduced based on the share of its caseload that consists of two-parent families.[60]
- The statute provides that a state may enter into a corrective compliance plan with HHS. A state that comes into compliance with the TANF work participation standards based on that plan can have its penalty either reduced or eliminated.
- The statute provides that the Secretary of HHS may determine that there was "reasonable cause" for a state to have failed its work standard. If the Secretary finds such reasonable cause, the state would not be penalized.

Thus, states are not necessarily penalized immediately for failing their work standards. HHS has not made a final penalty determination for states that did not meet the FY2011 standards.

THE 2002-2005 TANF REAUTHORIZATION DEBATE

Congress last debated TANF reauthorization proposals during the 2002 through 2005 period. President George W. Bush's TANF reauthorization proposal would have raised the participation standard percentage from 50% to 70%, ended the caseload reduction credit and replaced it with a credit for employed persons who leave the rolls, further limited counting pre-employment activities as a recipient's sole or primary activity, and raised the full hours standard to 40 hours per week but provided partial credit for fewer hours per week.[61]

The House passed bills incorporating most of the Bush Administration's proposals three times during the 2002-2005 periods.[62] (The major change not accepted by the House was ending the caseload reduction credit.) The Senate Finance Committee also reported three bills that raised the percentage standard, but they differed in terms of the form of the employment credit and would have expanded the ability of states to count pre-employment activities toward the work standard.[63]

Neither the House-passed nor the Senate Finance Committee approaches were adopted. Instead, the Deficit Reduction Act of 2005 (P.L. 109-171) made its changes to revise the caseload reduction credit, require HHS to issue regulations standardizing the definition of work activities, and require states to verify work participation.

If Congress would again consider raising participation standards, it would beg the question of *why* state participation rates have been fairly steady at 30%, with overall engagement basically steady at a little less than half of all work-eligible individuals. In 1995, as welfare reform was being considered, MDRC (the organization that evaluated many welfare-to-work programs) noted that the participation standard being contemplated at the time was much higher than those achieved in any program—including the most effective programs—that were tested up to that date.[64] As noted a number of times in this report, states have faced much-reduced standards because of credits. However, without additional research, and potentially experience, it is not known what higher participation standard is achievable for states and the consequences for state programs in achieving such a higher standard.

Looking Ahead: Welfare-to-Work Issues for Congress

The 2002-2005 debate did not result in a full-blown reauthorization of TANF. President Obama's Administration has not proposed a comprehensive reauthorization of TANF either, but instead provided some general principles to guide Congress's discussion:

> When Congress takes up reauthorization, the Administration will be prepared to work with lawmakers to strengthen the program's effectiveness in accomplishing its goals. This effort should include using performance indicators to drive program improvement and ensuring that states have the flexibility to engage recipients in the most effective activities to promote success in the workforce, including families with serious barriers to employment.[65]

This section will examine a number of issues that Congress might address in reassessing TANF and welfare-to-work issues. It

- discusses some changes in the economic and policy environments external to TANF that could affect future discussions;
- discusses the (brief) experience of subsidized employment programs funded through TANF in 2009 and 2010;
- examines some innovations in education and workforce programs that have yet to be tested in the context of welfare-to-work programs; and
- discusses the issues regarding the way TANF welfare-to-work programs are monitored and assessed.

Changing Employment Patterns (Again): The Case of Youth

Historically, welfare-to-work issues came to the fore, in part, because of changing employment patterns: the increase in labor force participation of women. "Pensions" to allow single mothers to stay home with their children gradually became out of sync with the prevailing labor force behavior of women not on assistance.

TANF defines an adult as a recipient age 20 and older for purposes of its work standards. For those ages 20 and older, the TANF work participation standards limit the counting of educational activities. However, the transition from childhood to adulthood has become longer and more complex, given changes in the economy that require longer periods of education to meet job demands.[66] Many policy initiatives enacted since the 1996 welfare reform law treat young adults as youth for the purposes of receiving benefits and services.[67]

During the post-welfare reform era, labor force participation and employment first increased, but then (after 2000) it declined for young women in total (on and off the benefit rolls) aged 20 to 24. Throughout the post-welfare reform period, enrollment for young women aged 20 to 24 in educational programs increased.

Table 11 shows the employment status of young adults (aged 20 to 24) for selected years from 1994 to 2011. In 2000, 73.1% of all women aged 20 to 24 participated in the labor force, with 67.9% of all women employed. These rates had declined some even before the onset of the 2007- 2009 recession. By 2007, the labor force participation rate for women aged 20 to 24 had declined to 70.1%, with the employment rate at 65.0% (about a 3 percentage point decline in both measures). These trends continued beyond the recession, with the labor force participation rate of women aged 20 to 24 falling to 67.8% in 2011 and the employment rate falling to 58.7% in that year.

Table 11. Employment Status of Young Adults (Aged 20 to 24), Selected Years 1994-2011 Monthly Averages Over the Year

	Labor Force Participation Rate			Employment Rate		
	All	**Men**	**Women**	**All**	**Men**	**Women**
1994	77.0%	83.1%	71.0%	69.5%	74.6%	64.5%
2000	77.8	82.6	73.1	72.2	76.6	67.9
2007	74.4	78.7	70.1	68.4	71.7	65.0
2011	71.3	74.7	67.8	60.8	63.0	58.7

Source: Congressional Research Service, based on data from the U.S. Bureau of Labor Statistics.

Note: Labor force participation rate is the percent of the population either employed or actively seeking employment. The employment rate is the percent of the population employed.

The decline in labor force participation for women aged 20 to 24 in the 2000s was accompanied by an increase in educational enrollment during the decade. **Table 12** shows the percentage of young adults enrolled in an educational program for selected years, 1994-2011, separately showing rates of enrollment by gender and age group. Educational enrollment increased for women throughout this period, even before 2000 as the labor force participation of women in this age group was also increasing. The rate at which women aged 20 and 21 were enrolled in an education program rose 9.1 percentage points, from 47.3% in 2000 to 56.4% in 2011. The rate at which women aged 22 to 24 were enrolled in an education program rose 6.7 percentage points during the decade, from 25.3% in 2000 to 32.0% in 2011.

Table 12. Enrollment in Educational Programs of Young Adults (Aged 20 to 24), Selected Years 1994-2011 October of Each Year

	Age 20 and 21			Age 22 through 24		
	All	Men	Women	All	Men	Women
1994	44.9%	42.7%	47.0%	24.1%	24.2%	23.9%
2000	44.1	41.0	47.3	24.6	23.9	25.3
2007	48.4	43.7	53.3	27.3	25.4	29.2
2011	52.7	49.2	56.4	31.1	30.3	32.0

Source: Congressional Research Service, based on data from the U.S. Census Bureau.

The changing employment and school enrollment patterns for the entire population of young women aged 20 to 24 have also been accompanied by the continuation of long-term trends of delay in the ages of marriage and in having a first child.

This could differentiate the young women on TANF (who are parents) from other members of their cohort. However, if the limits in counting education toward meeting TANF work participation standards result in state TANF programs curtailing the ability of recipients to engage in education, this could result in the TANF recipients becoming more educationally disadvantaged compared to their counterparts within their age cohort.[68]

Subsidized Employment

The American Recovery and Reinvestment Act of 2009 (P.L. 111-5) established within TANF an emergency contingency fund (ECF) that provided $5 billion for FY2009 and FY2010 to states, territories, and tribes to finance increased expenditures in three program areas: basic assistance, non-recurring short-term benefits, and subsidized employment.

Of the $5 billion provided by the ECF, $1.3 billion was used by states and tribes to finance increased expenditures for subsidized employment. The TANF ECF provided states and tribes with flexibility in designing their subsidized employment programs. Funds could be used to subsidize jobs for TANF assistance recipients or a broader population, though they were restricted to either low-income parents (including noncustodial parents) or youth. It is estimated that the TANF ECF helped support 281,000 subsidized job placements.[69]

About half of the subsidized job placements were for summer youth employment, with the other half for adult parents (including noncustodial parents).

The TANF ECF subsidized employment program was the largest since the 1970s. Given the flexibility afforded by TANF, states and tribes developed subsidized employment programs with wide variation in the populations served (assistance recipients or a broader population), types of jobs subsidized, amount and structure of the subsidy, and whether or not the subsidized job was a temporary measure or one leading to longer-lasting employment.

In many states, those in jobs subsidized by TANF ECF funds either never received cash assistance or the earnings provided to them by the job made them ineligible for TANF cash. Thus, these participants' families were not considered part of the caseload, nor would a state receive credit for them under the current TANF work participation standards. This is because a state only receives credit for engagement in subsidized employment for members of families receiving TANF assistance.

The TANF ECF expired on September 30, 2010. After the end of these extra funds, many states that operated subsidized employment programs either ended them or scaled them back substantially.

Policy Innovation

As previously mentioned, TANF work standards were informed by evaluations of policies tested in the 1980s and early 1990s. However, since then there have been a number of innovations in policies in the realm of education and training. These policies have not been tested within the context of welfare-to-work programs. Examples of such policies include the following:

- Career Pathway models, which combine education and work in a series of "steps," to provide advancement in jobs often within a specific economic sector (e.g., the health sector).[70]
- Programs that integrate basic adult education with college-level career and technical skills. As discussed above, NEWWS found some evidence of positive employment impacts for those who participate in adult basic education, obtain a GED, and then go on to post-secondary education. New program models have been developed that integrate adult basic and post-secondary education. An example of such a model is the I-Best program, operating in Washington state.[71]
- "Drop-out recovery" programs, which seek to re-engage those who left high school without a diploma in regular high school courses though in a separate setting devoted to meeting their needs. Some of these programs engage young adults (ages 20 and older).[72]
- Programs in community colleges that target low-income students (some of whom are parents) and provide financial incentives to students to complete semesters and persist in pursuing their educational goals. Other community college programs include "learning communities," where groups of disadvantaged students are grouped together in classes and support sessions.[73]

The TANF work participation standards do not preclude placing recipients of cash assistance in these types of programs. In some circumstances, participation in such programs might be countable toward the TANF participation standards.

However, states may be deterred from using such programs for cash assistance recipients if participation in them might exceed the durational limit (i.e., vocational educational training's one-year limit) or runs into other restrictions (i.e., adult basic education or ESL programs not being able to be counted).

Measuring State Performance

The Obama Administration's principles for reauthorization include working with Congress on performance indicators to drive program improvement. What those indicators are can have important implications for welfare-to-work programs.

TANF imposes its work requirements indirectly through its numerical performance measures— currently the numerical work participation standard.[74] It does this indirectly in part because of the program's place in the federal-state system.

TANF is a broad-based block grant to the states, with federal goals but a great deal of flexibility in meeting those goals. The TANF work participation numerical standards—and the potential financial penalties for meeting them—are to ensure that the states use their flexibility in ways consistent with the federal goals.

Noting that TANF work requirements are "indirect" is not to understate the role of the requirements or the importance of what measures are chosen to assess the effectiveness of state welfare-to-work efforts. The choice of measures can change behavior—in this case, the behavior of those who design and implement state TANF welfare-to-work rules.[75] Moreover, performance measures can have both intended and unintended effects. Their incentives could create incentives for states to behave such that they are "hitting the target but missing the point."[76]

An alternative to assessing state welfare-to-work performance based on the current numerical participation standards is to examine program outcomes. Examining outcomes is intuitively appealing. Outcomes such as job entry or leaving the welfare rolls with a job seem to measure more aptly whether TANF is achieving its goal of ending dependence of needy parents on government benefits through work.

However, outcome measures can have their own unintended consequences in terms of influencing the design of state programs. The most commonly cited unintended consequence is "cream skimming," improving performance outcomes through serving only those most likely to succeed and leaving behind the hardest-to-serve.

In addition, it can be argued that outcomes do not directly measure the effectiveness of a program. Some families would leave the cash assistance rolls even without the intervention of a program. The effectiveness of a welfare-to-work program can also be measured by whether the program made a difference: that is, did it result in more or speedier exits from the program and improve a participant's employment and earnings? That can only be measured by an evaluation of the impact of a program. There is research evidence that long-term impacts of labor force programs are not necessarily related to short-term outcome measures.[77]

Evaluation research, particularly using the oft-preferred random assignment method, also has its issues of cost, time taken to produce results, and even ethical concerns. Random assignment experiments usually can only tell whether a program had an impact or not, but not why.

Given the strengths and weaknesses of each approach to assessing TANF's welfare-to-work efforts, an option might be to have multiple measures of its effectiveness. Each measure could be placed in the context of its strengths and weaknesses and could be supplemented by additional information from other measures. Some measures might be more adaptable than others to changing economic and policy contexts.

CONCLUSION

TANF was the culmination of a decades-long evolution of assistance programs for disadvantaged children, most of whom lived with single mothers. It was created in 1996, and it reflected the policy concerns of the 1980s and 1990s in terms of welfare receipt and dependency.

The TANF work participation rules and policy goals reflect that time. They emphasized and set as policy goals work and job preparation aimed to move families as quickly as possible from welfare to work. It allowed only time-limited job search (maximum 12 weeks in a fiscal year), and de-emphasized longer-term education and training.

Though TANF emphasizes work, it does not require all families to have a working member or one who is participating in activities. The children in disadvantaged families—the families served by TANF assistance—live in varied settings, with many families in circumstances that do not lend themselves to participation in welfare-to-work programs.

In FY2011, out of 1.9 million families on the rolls in a typical month, about 306,500 were counted as "participating" by the official TANF work participation rate measure. Many families do not have a work-eligible member, as the parents are disabled and receiving SSI, the children are being cared for by non-parent relatives (e.g., grandparents), or the parents are ineligible immigrants.

The work participation standards have generally required that states engage less than 50% of all families with a work-eligible individual in countable activities.

In examining the economic trends among single parent families with children since 1996, a Congressional Research Service analysis concluded:

> In the years immediately preceding 1996 welfare reform, and in the years since, the nation's income safety net has been transformed into one supporting work. Cash-welfare work requirements, the end of cash welfare as an open-ended entitlement by limiting the duration that individuals may receive federally funded benefits, and expanded earnings and family income supplements administered through the federal income tax system have helped to change the dynamics between work and welfare. The transformed system has helped to both reduce single mothers' reliance on traditional cash welfare and reduce poverty among their children.[78]

However, in the 2000s, *even before the onset of the 2007-2009 recession*, the decline in the cash assistance rolls slowed, and child poverty began to increase. Most measures of welfare-to-work activity discussed in this report—the official participation rate and a broader measure of the percentage of work-eligible individuals in activities—were all fairly stagnant over the FY2002-FY2011 period.

Additionally, the base of knowledge about what type of welfare-to-work program is effective for whom is little changed from the time welfare reform was enacted. The period of innovation and experimentation that preceded welfare reform produced evidence that helped shape TANF: experiments showed mandatory work requirements can increase employment and reduce welfare receipt, and earnings supplements can also serve as incentives to work in addition to raising incomes and even improving the development trajectory of children in participating families. Post-welfare reform research has generated no similar breakthroughs as yet. A question facing policy makers is whether the status quo regarding TANF welfare-to-work efforts is satisfactory, or whether (and how) policy makers may want to improve program performance or address changing needs or opportunities. Another question facing policy makers is whether the current structure of assessing welfare-to-work programs propels or impedes program innovations that can address changing circumstances among the disadvantaged. TANF evolved from a program focused on cash welfare to a broad-based block grant that can fund a wide range of benefits and services related to either ameliorating or addressing the causes of child poverty. Yet TANF's work participation rate remains the major official assessment of how well the program is doing. Policy makers also face questions about whether the sole focus of assessing TANF ought to be its welfare-to-work performance, or whether attention should also be paid to how well TANF does in terms of meeting other goals related to improving the circumstances of families with children.

APPENDIX A. ADDITIONAL TABLES

Table A-1. Effective TANF Work Participation Standards for All Families by State: FY2002-FY2011 Effective Standards are After Caseload Reduction Credits, Including Excess MOE Credits

State	2002	2003	2004	2005	2006	2007	2008	2009	2010	2011
Alabama	0.0%	0.0%	0.0%	0.0%	0.0%	0.0%	0.0%	0.0%	0.0%	0.0%
Alaska	8.7	11.1	6.9	4.8	6.8	32.5	25.8	21.4	21.4	21.4
Arizona	4.8	13.1	19.6	24.0	11.6	7.3	0.0	0.0	0.0	0.0
Arkansas	0.0	3.3	4.3	3.9	2.7	0.0	0.0	0.0	0.0	0.0
California	6.7	5.8	3.9	4.5	5.1	32.3	29.0	29.0	29.0	29.0
Colorado	0.0	0.0	0.0	0.0	0.0	15.1	0.0	0.0	0.0	0.0
Connecticut	21.0	20.3	20.2	23.4	23.4	12.7	0.0	0.0	0.0	0.0
Delaware	6.7	10.2	12.5	17.6	18.2	26.1	0.0	0.0	0.0	0.0
District of Columbia	11.2	11.5	13.3	15.3	14.4	32.5	31.9	31.9	26.0	31.9
Florida	0.0	0.0	0.0	0.0	0.0	2.4	0.0	0.0	0.0	0.0
Georgia	0.0	0.0	4.3	5.9	0.0	26.0	13.8	12.3	0.3	0.0
Hawaii	26.6	20.0	16.4	12.1	0.0	20.8	0.0	0.0	0.0	0.0
Idaho	15.9	20.0	34.5	27.9	28.5	43.1	38.1	30.6	30.6	30.6
Illinois	0.0	0.0	0.0	0.0	0.0	44.7	0.0	0.0	0.0	0.0
Indiana	15.4	28.9	35.4	33.4	27.1	46.5	11.3	11.3	11.3	11.3
Iowa	6.4	7.3	8.8	11.0	17.3	25.7	24.0	24.0	24.0	24.0
Kansas	38.4	41.7	37.6	38.8	38.8	11.5	0.0	0.0	0.0	0.0
Kentucky	2.9	4.5	6.2	10.1	11.9	41.7	36.6	31.9	31.5	29.4
Louisiana	0.0	0.0	0.0	0.0	0.0	24.0	17.4	15.2	13.6	15.2
Maine	1.9	2.5	0.0	1.1	2.9	31.4	47.5	47.5	47.5	47.5

State	2002	2003	2004	2005	2006	2007	2008	2009	2010	2011
Maryland	6.2	6.5	6.6	6.5	5.2	34.1	31.7	31.7	31.7	31.7
Massachusetts	0.8	4.9	6.3	8.4	8.5	14.3	0.0	0.0	0.0	0.0
Michigan	0.0	0.0	0.0	0.0	0.0	30.5	50.0	27.8	25.2	27.8
Minnesota	12.9	14.8	18.6	18.8	14.9	44.6	0.0	0.0	0.0	0.0
Mississippi	12.5	12.6	17.1	5.4	4.1	33.5	22.2	20.2	20.2	20.2
Missouri	5.7	5.0	3.7	4.5	2.8	7.4	14.9	14.9	14.9	14.9
Montana	0.0	2.0	10.8	13.2	16.3	26.1	26.0	25.8	25.8	25.8
Nebraska	17.6	24.2	28.7	28.6	31.1	23.0	0.0	0.0	0.0	0.0
Nevada	4.1	26.2	31.8	10.3	10.7	38.6	34.5	31.2	28.8	31.2
New Hampshire	2.4	6.1	7.8	7.4	8.4	9.5	0.0	0.0	0.0	0.0
New Jersey	0.0	0.0	0.0	0.0	0.0	0.0	0.0	0.0	0.0	0.0
New Mexico	8.3	8.4	8.2	12.0	13.2	46.2	15.2	15.2	15.2	15.2
New York	0.0	0.0	0.0	0.0	0.0	13.8	11.5	11.5	11.5	11.5
North Carolina	0.0	0.0	0.0	0.0	0.0	22.1	0.0	0.0	0.0	0.0
North Dakota	7.5	12.0	14.7	8.8	4.8	44.0	23.1	20.8	20.8	20.8
Ohio	0.0	0.0	9.7	15.7	19.1	46.2	42.0	42.0	42.0	42.0
Oklahoma	2.9	0.0	0.0	0.0	0.0	34.6	28.8	20.6	20.6	20.6
Oregon	0.0	0.0	0.0	0.0	0.3	45.1	45.4	45.4	45.4	45.4
Pennsylvania	0.0	0.0	0.0	0.0	0.0	42.0	19.7	15.8	14.3	15.8
Puerto Rico	0.0	3.1	0.0	0.0	0.0	44.6	40.3	23.5	23.5	23.5
Rhode Island	22.9	19.2	15.4	13.1	10.7	8.0	0.0	0.0	0.0	0.0
South Carolina	0.7	2.4	3.0	3.0	3.3	29.0	0.0	0.0	0.0	0.0
South Dakota	9.3	12.4	11.7	10.9	13.7	50.0	50.0	50.0	50.0	50.0
Tennessee	7.8	11.6	11.6	19.6	19.1	35.5	0.0	0.0	0.0	0.0
Texas	0.0	0.0	0.9	0.0	0.0	31.2	19.9	10.8	4.7	7.8
Utah	11.7	17.0	24.6	17.8	27.3	32.6	10.1	5.4	5.4	5.4

Table A-1. (Continued)

State	2002	2003	2004	2005	2006	2007	2008	2009	2010	2011
Vermont	8.8	7.1	5.7	5.5	2.4	23.0	11.1	11.1	11.1	11.1
Virginia	0.0	0.0	0.0	0.1	0.8	36.0	38.5	37.8	37.8	37.8
Washington	7.0	8.2	8.8	6.9	10.7	11.1	0.0	0.0	0.0	0.0
West Virginia	0.0	0.0	0.0	0.0	0.0	39.2	26.3	17.4	17.4	17.4
Wisconsin	0.0	0.0	0.4	1.3	0.0	30.9	0.0	0.0	0.0	0.0
Wyoming	0.0	0.0	0.0	0.0	0.0	47.3	35.3	34.2	34.2	34.2
Guam	50.0	50.0	50.0	50.0	50.0	50.0	50.0	50.0	50.0	50.0
Virgin Islands	6.5	0.0	0.0	0.0	0.0	0.0	0.0	0.0	0.0	0.0
Number of States with Effective (After-Credit) TANF Work Participation Standard Equal to:										
Zero	21	20	18	17	19	4	22	22	22	23
1%-9.9%	21	15	17	16	14	5	0	1	3	2
10.0%-19.9%	7	11	11	14	14	6	10	10	8	8
20.0%-29.9%	3	6	3	4	4	10	8	9	11	10
30.0%-39.9%	1	0	4	2	2	15	7	7	5	6
40.0%-49.9%	0	1	0	0	0	12	4	3	3	3
50%	1	1	1	1	1	2	3	2	2	2

Source: Congressional Research Service, based on data from the U.S. Department of Health and Human Services.

Table A-2. TANF Work Participation Rates by State: Official Rates (Including Grandfathered Waivers), FY2002-FY2011

State	2002	2003	2004	2005	2006	2007	2008	2009	2010	2011
Alabama	37.3%	37.1%	37.9%	38.6%	41.6%	34.0%	37.4%	32.4%	37.1%	40.6%
Alaska	39.6	41.1	43.6	45.7	45.6	46.8	42.8	37.2	33.3	38.5
Arizona	25.9	13.4	25.5	30.3	29.6	30.0	27.8	27.1	29.1	33.5
Arkansas	21.4	22.4	27.3	28.3	27.9	35.3	38.8	37.1	34.1	36.1
California	27.3	24.0	23.1	25.9	22.2	22.3	25.1	26.8	26.2	27.8
Colorado	35.9	32.5	34.7	25.8	30.0	27.3	32.3	37.8	33.6	32.1
Connecticut	26.6	30.6	24.3	33.8	30.8	28.8	25.3	34.4	37.2	59.2
Delaware	25.8	18.2	22.1	22.6	25.3	32.7	48.8	37.5	38.8	39.0
District of Columbia	16.4	23.1	18.2	23.5	17.1	35.0	49.6	23.5	15.0	20.0
Florida	30.4	33.1	40.4	38.0	41.0	64.2	42.4	46.1	47.5	44.8
Georgia	8.2	10.9	24.8	57.2	64.9	54.2	59.0	57.1	67.5	66.0
Hawaii	58.8	65.8	70.5	35.5	37.3	28.7	34.4	40.3	47.6	51.2
Idaho	40.7	43.7	41.0	39.9	44.2	53.0	59.5	52.0	49.5	51.6
Illinois	58.4	57.8	46.1	43.0	53.0	55.5	42.6	49.3	49.1	44.1
Indiana	62.6	40.3	36.3	30.9	26.7	27.5	29.4	17.5	19.2	19.5
Iowa	51.2	45.1	50.0	47.8	39.0	40.2	41.1	35.4	34.8	37.6
Kansas	84.8	87.9	88.0	86.7	77.2	12.8	19.6	23.9	27.2	27.6
Kentucky	32.4	32.8	38.1	39.7	44.6	38.2	38.0	37.3	46.4	52.5
Louisiana	38.7	34.6	35.4	34.6	38.4	42.2	40.0	34.4	27.4	25.3
Maine	44.5	27.7	32.1	28.3	26.6	21.9	11.4	16.8	19.7	19.1
Maryland	8.3	9.1	16.0	20.5	44.5	46.7	36.9	44.0	40.7	43.6
Massachusetts	60.9	61.0	60.0	59.9	13.6	17.0	44.7	47.5	22.2	7.3

Table A-2. (Continued)

State	2002	2003	2004	2005	2006	2007	2008	2009	2010	2011
Michigan	28.9	25.3	24.5	22.0	21.6	28.0	33.6	27.9	22.8	26.6
Minnesota	40.4	25.0	26.8	28.9	30.3	28.1	29.9	29.8	40.2	43.9
Mississippi	18.5	17.2	21.0	22.6	35.5	61.9	63.2	67.5	66.3	65.1
Missouri	25.4	28.0	19.5	20.0	18.7	14.0	14.2	13.2	17.5	14.4
Montana	84.2	85.9	92.7	83.1	79.2	46.4	44.2	44.2	51.6	49.0
Nebraska	28.1	33.4	34.5	31.8	32.0	23.0	51.2	50.3	49.5	51.9
Nevada	21.6	22.3	34.5	42.3	47.8	34.0	42.1	39.4	37.6	37.8
New Hampshire	41.8	28.2	30.2	24.6	24.1	42.0	47.4	46.5	46.6	49.2
New Jersey	36.4	35.0	34.6	29.0	29.2	33.0	18.9	20.1	19.9	17.5
New Mexico	42.7	42.0	46.2	41.6	42.3	36.4	37.5	43.1	42.5	42.0
New York	38.5	37.1	37.8	35.2	37.8	38.0	37.3	33.4	35.0	33.8
North Carolina	27.4	25.3	31.4	27.5	32.4	32.4	24.5	32.3	37.1	49.5
North Dakota	30.4	27.0	25.3	31.4	51.9	58.7	50.2	61.0	68.7	67.6
Ohio	56.3	62.3	65.2	58.3	54.9	23.7	24.5	23.3	23.1	27.3
Oklahoma	26.7	29.2	33.2	34.0	32.9	38.1	29.2	23.0	24.3	24.9
Oregon	61.1	60.0	32.1	14.9	15.2	14.7	24.1	9.5	8.4	14.1
Pennsylvania	10.4	9.9	7.1	15.2	26.1	48.9	38.6	45.8	46.0	39.3
Puerto Rico	5.6	6.1	7.5	13.1	13.1	8.2	11.6	8.7	8.6	11.8
Rhode Island	24.6	24.3	23.7	24.2	24.9	26.8	17.5	13.8	12.0	11.0
South Carolina	52.4	54.3	53.7	54.3	49.5	53.3	51.7	45.1	37.2	37.3
South Dakota	42.5	46.1	54.8	57.5	57.9	53.5	62.2	59.4	61.4	56.7
Tennessee	41.2	42.7	50.6	52.1	57.2	45.9	25.2	25.5	26.5	27.4
Texas	30.8	28.1	34.2	38.9	42.0	34.6	29.3	37.0	36.1	39.4
Utah	27.9	28.1	26.2	30.3	42.5	49.8	37.6	32.6	33.8	26.3

State	2002	2003	2004	2005	2006	2007	2008	2009	2010	2011
Vermont	21.4	24.3	24.9	22.4	22.2	22.4	23.2	29.0	34.9	40.5
Virginia	42.9	44.6	50.1	46.3	53.9	43.5	45.4	44.3	42.9	44.0
Washington	49.8	46.2	35.4	38.6	36.1	25.4	18.3	23.0	24.2	15.0
West Virginia	19.2	14.2	11.7	16.3	26.2	15.4	17.6	19.6	25.9	32.9
Wisconsin	69.4	67.2	61.3	44.3	36.2	36.7	37.1	39.9	42.5	37.6
Wyoming	82.9	83.0	77.8	82.1	77.2	65.4	50.5	61.3	63.4	68.7
Guam	0.0	0.0	0.0	0.0	0.0	2.5	0.0	0.0	1.0	2.3
Virgin Islands	17.7	5.0	10.6	16.9	14.5	17.1	15.5	7.1	9.2	8.4
Number of States with Participation Rates Equal to:										
0%-9.9%	4	5	3	1	1	2	1	4	4	3
10.0%-19.9%	5	5	5	5	6	6	9	5	6	8
20.0%-29.9%	14	16	13	16	13	13	12	12	11	9
30.0%-39.9%	10	9	16	16	13	14	12	15	14	13
40.0%-49.9%	9	9	5	7	11	10	12	11	13	11
50% or more	12	10	12	9	10	9	8	7	6	10

Source: Congressional Research Service, based on data from the U.S. Department of Health and Human Services.

Table A-3. TANF Work Participation Rates for All Families Excluding the Effects of Grandfathered Waivers by State: FY2002-FY2011

State	2002	2003	2004	2005	2006	2007	2008	2009	2010	2011
Alabama	37.3%	37.1%	37.9%	38.6%	41.6%	34.0%	37.4%	32.4%	37.1%	40.6%
Alaska	39.6	41.1	43.6	45.7	45.6	46.8	42.8	37.2	33.3	38.5
Arizona	25.9	13.4	25.5	30.3	29.6	30.0	27.8	27.1	29.1	33.5
Arkansas	21.4	22.4	27.3	28.3	27.9	35.3	38.8	37.1	34.1	36.1
California	27.3	24.0	23.1	25.9	22.2	22.3	25.1	26.8	26.2	27.8
Colorado	35.9	32.5	34.7	25.8	30.0	27.3	32.3	37.8	33.6	32.1
Connecticut	26.6	30.6	24.3	33.8	30.8	28.8	25.3	34.4	37.2	59.2
Delaware	11.7	18.2	22.1	22.6	25.3	32.7	48.8	37.5	38.8	39.0
District of Columbia	16.4	23.1	18.2	23.5	17.1	35.0	49.6	23.5	15.0	20.0
Florida	30.4	33.1	40.4	38.0	41.0	64.2	42.4	46.1	47.5	44.8
Georgia	8.2	10.9	24.8	57.2	64.9	54.2	59.0	57.1	67.5	66.0
Hawaii	32.5	34.6	40.3	35.5	37.3	28.7	34.4	40.3	47.6	51.2
Idaho	40.7	43.7	41.0	39.9	44.2	53.0	59.5	52.0	49.5	51.6
Illinois	58.4	57.8	46.1	43.0	53.0	55.5	42.6	49.3	49.1	44.1
Indiana	45.3	40.3	36.3	30.9	26.7	27.5	29.4	17.5	19.2	19.5
Iowa	51.2	45.1	50.0	47.8	39.0	40.2	41.1	35.4	34.8	37.6
Kansas	37.6	32.4	88.0	86.7	77.2	12.8	19.6	23.9	27.2	27.6
Kentucky	32.4	32.8	38.1	39.7	44.6	38.2	38.0	37.3	46.4	52.5
Louisiana	38.7	34.6	35.4	34.6	38.4	42.2	40.0	34.4	27.4	25.3
Maine	44.5	27.7	32.1	28.3	26.6	21.9	11.4	16.8	19.7	19.1
Maryland	8.3	9.1	16.0	20.5	44.5	46.7	36.9	44.0	40.7	43.6
Massachusetts	9.2	8.4	10.3	12.6	13.6	17.0	44.7	47.5	22.2	7.3
Michigan	28.9	25.3	24.5	22.0	21.6	28.0	33.6	27.9	22.8	26.6

State	2002	2003	2004	2005	2006	2007	2008	2009	2010	2011
Minnesota	31.2	25.0	26.8	28.9	30.3	28.1	29.9	29.8	40.2	43.9
Mississippi	18.5	17.2	21.0	22.5	35.5	61.9	63.2	67.5	66.3	65.1
Missouri	25.4	28.0	19.5	20.0	18.7	14.0	14.2	13.2	17.5	14.4
Montana	37.9	37.4	86.7	83.1	79.2	46.4	44.2	44.2	51.6	49.0
Nebraska	22.8	29.4	34.5	31.8	32.0	23.0	51.2	50.3	49.5	51.9
Nevada	21.6	22.3	34.5	42.3	47.8	34.0	42.1	39.4	37.6	37.8
New Hampshire	32.6	28.2	30.2	24.6	24.1	42.0	47.4	46.5	46.6	49.2
New Jersey	36.4	35.0	34.6	29.0	29.2	33.0	18.9	20.1	19.9	17.5
New Mexico	42.7	42.0	46.2	41.6	42.3	36.4	37.5	43.1	42.5	42.0
New York	38.5	37.1	37.8	35.2	37.8	38.0	37.3	33.4	35.0	33.8
North Carolina	27.4	25.3	31.4	27.5	32.4	32.4	24.5	32.3	37.1	49.5
North Dakota	30.4	27.0	25.3	31.4	51.9	58.7	50.2	61.0	68.7	67.6
Ohio	56.1	62.2	65.2	58.3	54.9	23.7	24.5	23.3	23.1	27.3
Oklahoma	26.7	29.2	33.2	34.0	32.9	38.1	29.2	23.0	24.3	24.9
Oregon	8.0	14.7	32.1	14.9	15.2	14.7	24.1	9.5	8.4	14.1
Pennsylvania	10.4	9.9	7.1	15.2	26.1	48.9	38.6	45.8	46.0	39.3
Puerto Rico	5.6	6.1	7.5	13.1	13.1	8.2	11.6	8.7	8.6	11.8
Rhode Island	24.6	24.3	23.7	24.2	24.9	26.8	17.5	13.8	12.0	11.0
South Carolina	30.2	28.6	53.7	54.3	49.5	53.3	51.7	45.1	37.2	37.3
South Dakota	42.5	46.1	54.8	57.5	57.9	53.5	62.2	59.4	61.4	56.7
Tennessee	14.3	13.4	13.0	14.3	16.8	45.9	25.2	25.5	26.5	27.4
Texas	21.1	28.1	34.2	38.9	42.0	34.6	29.3	37.0	36.1	39.4
Utah	27.9	28.1	26.2	30.3	42.5	49.8	37.6	32.6	33.8	26.3
Vermont	21.4	24.3	24.9	22.4	22.2	22.4	23.2	29.0	34.9	40.5
Virginia	22.6	29.9	50.1	46.3	53.9	43.5	45.4	44.3	42.9	44.0

Table A-3. (Continued)

State	2002	2003	2004	2005	2006	2007	2008	2009	2010	2011
Washington	49.8	46.2	35.4	38.6	36.1	25.4	18.3	23.0	24.2	15.0
West Virginia	19.2	14.2	11.7	16.3	26.2	15.4	17.6	19.6	25.9	32.9
Wisconsin	69.4	67.2	61.3	44.3	36.2	36.7	37.1	39.9	42.5	37.6
Wyoming	82.9	83.0	77.8	82.1	77.2	65.4	50.5	61.3	63.4	68.7
Guam	0.0	0.0	0.0	0.0	0.0	2.5	0.0	0.0	1.0	2.3
Virgin Islands	17.7	5.0	10.6	16.9	14.5	17.1	15.5	7.1	9.2	8.4
States with Participation Rates Equal to:										
0%-9.9%	6	6	3	1	1	2	1	4	4	3
10.0%-19.9%	7	7	7	7	7	6	9	5	6	8
20.0%-29.9%	15	19	13	16	13	13	12	12	11	9
30.0%-39.9%	15	11	16	16	13	14	12	15	14	13
40.0%-49.9%	6	7	6	7	11	10	12	11	13	11
50.0% and more	5	4	9	7	9	9	8	7	6	10

Source: Congressional Research Service, based on data from the U.S. Department of Health and Human Services.

Table A-4. TANF Effective Work Participation Standards and Work Participation Rates: FY2011

State	All-Family Standard			Two-Parent Standard				
	Effective (After Credit) Standard	Participation Rate	Met Standard?	Effective (After Credit) Standards		Participation Rate		Met Standard?
Alabama	0.0%	40.6%	Yes		0.0%		34.3%	Yes
Alaska	21.4	38.5	Yes		51.0		62.6	Yes
Arizona	0.0	33.5	Yes		30.5		73	Yes
Arkansas	0.0	36.1	Yes		0.0		24.8	Yes
California	29.0	27.8	No		0.0		33.9	Yes
Colorado	0.0	32.1	Yes		4.1		23.6	Yes
Connecticut	0.0	59.2	Yes	NA		NA		NA
Delaware	0.0	39.0	Yes	NA		NA		NA
District of Columbia	31.9	20.0	No	NA		NA		NA
Florida	0.0	44.8	Yes		0.0		56.1	Yes
Georgia	0.0	66.0	Yes	NA		NA		NA
Hawaii	0.0	51.2	Yes		9.6		63.7	Yes
Idaho	30.6	51.6	Yes	NA		NA		NA
Illinois	0.0	44.1	Yes	NA		NA		NA
Indiana	11.3	19.5	Yes		0.0		16	Yes
Iowa	24.0	37.6	Yes		0.0		32.6	Yes
Kansas	0.0	27.6	Yes		0.0		31	Yes
Kentucky	29.4	52.5	Yes		40.0		49.6	Yes
Louisiana	15.2	25.3	Yes	NA		NA		NA
Maine	47.5	19.1	No		87.5		18.7	No
Maryland	31.7	43.6	Yes	NA		NA		NA

Table A-4. (Continued)

State	All-Family Standard			Two-Parent Standard				
	Effective (After Credit) Standard	Participation Rate	Met Standard?	Effective (After Credit) Standards		Participation Rate		Met Standard?
Massachusetts	0.0	7.3	Yes	NA		NA		NA
Michigan	27.8	26.6	No	NA		NA		NA
Minnesota	0.0	43.9	Yes	NA		NA		NA
Mississippi	20.2	65.1	Yes	NA		NA		NA
Missouri	14.9	14.4	No	NA		NA		NA
Montana	25.8	49.0	Yes		19.7		58.6	Yes
Nebraska	0.0	51.9	Yes	NA		NA		NA
Nevada	31.2	37.8	Yes		71.2		46.3	No
New Hampshire	0.0	49.2	Yes	NA		NA		NA
New Jersey	0.0	17.5	Yes	NA		NA		NA
New Mexico	15.2	42.0	Yes		0.0		49.2	Yes
New York	11.5	33.8	Yes	NA		NA		NA
North Carolina	0.0	49.5	Yes		0.0		66.7	Yes
North Dakota	20.8	67.6	Yes	NA		NA		NA
Ohio	42.0	27.3	No		10.1		29.5	Yes
Oklahoma	20.6	24.9	Yes	NA		NA		NA
Oregon	45.4	14.1	No		85.4		7.4	No
Pennsylvania	15.8	39.3	Yes		13.0		61.6	Yes
Puerto Rico	23.5	11.8	No	NA			NA	NA
Rhode Island	0.0	11.0	Yes		30.7		8.3	No
South Carolina	0.0	37.3	Yes	NA		NA		NA

State	All-Family Standard			Two-Parent Standard				
	Effective (After Credit) Standard	Participation Rate	Met Standard?	Effective (After Credit) Standards		Participation Rate		Met Standard?
South Dakota	50.0	56.7	Yes	NA		NA		NA
Tennessee	0.0	27.4	Yes		0.0		0	Yes
Texas	7.8	39.4	Yes	NA		NA		NA
Utah	5.4	26.3	Yes	NA		NA		NA
Vermont	11.1	40.5	Yes		0.0		45.7	Yes
Virginia	37.8	44.0	Yes	NA		NA		NA
Washington	0.0	15.0	Yes		0.0		14.8	Yes
West Virginia	17.4	32.9	Yes	NA		NA		NA
Wisconsin	0.0	37.6	Yes		0.0		22	Yes
Wyoming	34.2	68.7	Yes		25.3		80.4	Yes
Guam	50.0	2.3	No		90.0		1.5	No
Virgin Islands	0.0	8.4	Yes	NA		NA		NA
Number of states that:								
Met standard			45					22
Failed standard			9					5
Not applicable			0					27

Source: Congressional Research Service, based on data from the U.S. Department of Health and Human Services.

Table A-5. TANF Families Receiving Assistance, by Type of Family and State: FY2011 As a Percentage of All TANF Families Receiving Assistance

State	No Work-Eligible Individual	Single-Parent Family	Two-Parent Family	Total
Alabama	35.0%	64.3%	0.7%	100.0%
Alaska	29.8	60.5	9.6	100.0
Arizona	40.7	55.9	3.3	100.0
Arkansas	38.6	58.7	2.7	100.0
California	34.1	54.7	11.2	100.0
Colorado	41.8	50.7	7.5	100.0
Connecticut	46.0	54.0	0.0	100.0
Delaware	54.2	45.2	0.6	100.0
District of Columbia	26.5	73.5	0.0	100.0
Florida	71.6	26.4	2.0	100.0
Georgia	81.8	18.2	0.0	100.0
Hawaii	26.4	53.8	19.8	100.0
Idaho	89.3	10.7	0.0	100.0
Illinois	50.1	49.9	0.0	100.0
Indiana	33.2	60.4	6.4	100.0
Iowa	27.7	66.3	6.0	100.0
Kansas	27.6	63.0	9.4	100.0
Kentucky	60.5	36.9	2.6	100.0
Louisiana	64.3	35.7	0.0	100.0
Maine	16.4	70.2	13.3	100.0
Maryland	40.7	59.3	0.0	100.0

State	No Work-Eligible Individual	Single-Parent Family	Two-Parent Family	Total
Massachusetts	38.7	60.3	1.0	100.0
Michigan	28.5	71.5	0.0	100.0
Minnesota	42.9	57.1	0.0	100.0
Mississippi	41.2	58.8	0.0	100.0
Missouri	22.2	77.8	0.0	100.0
Montana	39.0	51.1	9.9	100.0
Nebraska	46.1	53.9	0.0	100.0
Nevada	46.0	44.1	9.9	100.0
New Hampshire	42.1	55.5	2.4	100.0
New Jersey	27.6	72.4	0.0	100.0
New Mexico	34.2	56.6	9.2	100.0
New York	40.7	57.9	1.4	100.0
North Carolina	70.9	27.7	1.4	100.0
North Dakota	26.8	73.2	0.0	100.0
Ohio	47.0	45.3	7.7	100.0
Oklahoma	57.9	42.1	0.0	100.0
Oregon	24.1	65.2	10.7	100.0
Pennsylvania	37.0	61.2	1.9	100.0
Rhode Island	34.4	57.7	7.9	100.0
South Carolina	14.7	85.3	0.0	100.0
South Dakota	67.2	32.8	0.0	100.0
Tennessee	32.2	65.7	2.0	100.0
Texas	65.9	34.1	0.0	100.0
Utah	46.9	53.1	0.0	100.0
Vermont	40.4	47.5	12.1	100.0

Table A-5. (Continued)

State	No Work-Eligible Individual	Single-Parent Family	Two-Parent Family	Total
Virginia	36.9	63.1	0.0	100.0
Washington	39.4	50.6	10.0	100.0
West Virginia	46.9	53.1	0.0	100.0
Wisconsin	45.7	51.7	2.6	100.0
Wyoming	70.2	28.4	1.5	100.0
Guam	51.6	33.2	15.2	100.0
Puerto Rico	10.8	89.2	0.0	100.0
Virgin Islands	14.0	86.0	0.0	100.0
Total	39.1	55.2	5.7	100.0

Source: Congressional Research Service (CRS) tabulations of the FY2011 TANF National Data Files.

Table A-6. TANF Families Receiving Assistance, by Work Participation Rate Status and State: FY2011

As a Percentage of All TANF Families Receiving Assistance

State	No Work-Eligible Individual	Disregarded from the Rate	In Participation Rate	Total
Alabama	35.0%	10.9%	54.2%	100.0%
Alaska	29.8	8.6	61.6	100.0
Arizona	40.7	7.7	51.6	100.0
Arkansas	38.6	13.4	47.9	100.0
California	34.1	4.3	61.6	100.0
Colorado	41.8	6.7	51.5	100.0
Connecticut	46.0	12.5	41.5	100.0
Delaware	54.2	11.6	34.2	100.0
District of Columbia	26.5	18.0	55.5	100.0
Florida	71.6	5.2	23.2	100.0
Georgia	81.8	2.9	15.3	100.0
Hawaii	26.4	5.2	68.4	100.0
Idaho	89.3	1.8	8.9	100.0
Illinois	50.1	3.6	46.4	100.0
Indiana	33.2	10.0	56.8	100.0
Iowa	27.7	5.8	66.6	100.0
Kansas	27.6	11.5	60.9	100.0
Kentucky	60.5	7.8	31.7	100.0
Louisiana	64.3	4.2	31.5	100.0
Maine	16.4	2.0	81.6	100.0

Table A-6. (Continued)

State	No Work-Eligible Individual	Disregarded from the Rate	In Participation Rate	Total
Maryland	40.7	12.1	47.2	100.0
Massachusetts	38.7	10.1	51.1	100.0
Michigan	28.5	15.5	56.0	100.0
Minnesota	42.9	14.3	42.8	100.0
Mississippi	41.2	13.4	45.4	100.0
Missouri	22.2	10.9	66.9	100.0
Montana	39.0	19.4	41.6	100.0
Nebraska	46.1	6.4	47.4	100.0
Nevada	46.0	3.1	50.9	100.0
New Hampshire	42.1	12.4	45.5	100.0
New Jersey	27.6	9.1	63.3	100.0
New Mexico	34.2	10.0	55.8	100.0
New York	40.7	4.2	55.1	100.0
North Carolina	70.9	6.9	22.1	100.0
North Dakota	26.8	34.1	39.1	100.0
Ohio	47.0	6.9	46.1	100.0
Oklahoma	57.9	7.8	34.3	100.0
Oregon	24.1	7.8	68.1	100.0
Pennsylvania	37.0	12.3	50.7	100.0
Rhode Island	34.4	7.3	58.3	100.0
South Carolina	14.7	17.8	67.4	100.0
South Dakota	67.2	8.6	24.1	100.0

State	No Work-Eligible Individual	Disregarded from the Rate	In Participation Rate	Total
Tennessee	32.2	14.0	53.8	100.0
Texas	65.9	2.5	31.6	100.0
Utah	46.9	0.0	53.1	100.0
Vermont	40.4	10.4	49.2	100.0
Virginia	36.9	9.9	53.2	100.0
Washington	39.4	9.9	50.7	100.0
West Virginia	46.9	9.5	43.6	100.0
Wisconsin	45.7	12.7	41.7	100.0
Wyoming	70.2	5.0	24.8	100.0
Guam	51.6	2.3	46.1	100.0
Puerto Rico	10.8	7.2	82.1	100.0
Virgin Islands	14.0	0.0	86.0	100.0
Total	39.1	7.4	53.5	100.0

Source: Congressional Research Service tabulations of the FY2011 TANF National Data Files.

Table A-7. TANF Families Included in the Work Participation Rate, by Family Type and State, FY2011
Family Type Based on Minimum Hours Requirements Under the TANF Work Participation Standards

State	Teen Parents without a High School Diploma	Single Parents with a Child Under the Age of 6	Single Parents All Children Age 6 and Older	Two-Parent Family Not Receiving Federally Funded Child Care	Two-Parent Family Receiving Federally Funded Child Care	Totals
Alabama	1.9%	64.4%	32.4%	1.2%	0.1%	100.0%
Alaska	2.6	50.4	33.0	13.1	0.8	100.0
Arizona	2.3	55.7	36.3	5.3	0.3	100.0
Arkansas	4.0	65.4	25.2	4.7	0.6	100.0
California	1.9	41.4	38.6	18.1	0.0	100.0
Colorado	6.5	49.2	30.0	14.3	0.0	100.0
Connecticut	5.5	68.2	26.4	0.0	0.0	100.0
Delaware	1.9	68.8	27.6	1.4	0.2	100.0
District of Columbia	1.6	72.8	25.7	0.0	0.0	100.0
Florida	1.4	58.7	31.3	6.3	2.3	100.0
Georgia	8.4	67.6	24.0	0.0	0.0	100.0
Hawaii	0.5	41.6	29.1	28.1	0.8	100.0
Idaho	4.6	67.8	27.6	0.0	0.0	100.0
Illinois	6.0	67.2	26.9	0.0	0.0	100.0
Indiana	3.2	50.8	34.9	10.6	0.5	100.0
Iowa	3.8	46.9	40.6	8.8	0.0	100.0
Kansas	3.5	45.9	35.4	14.5	0.8	100.0
Kentucky	4.8	61.4	25.8	7.2	0.9	100.0

State	Teen Parents without a High School Diploma	Single Parents with a Child Under the Age of 6	Single Parents All Children Age 6 and Older	Two-Parent Family Not Receiving Federally Funded Child Care	Two-Parent Family Receiving Federally Funded Child Care	Totals
Louisiana	4.8	71.2	24.0	0.0	0.0	100.0
Maine	1.6	37.4	44.6	16.2	0.1	100.0
Maryland	3.1	65.2	31.7	0.0	0.0	100.0
Massachusetts	2.7	58.4	37.0	1.9	0.0	100.0
Michigan	2.4	57.5	40.1	0.0	0.0	100.0
Minnesota	8.1	51.9	40.0	0.0	0.0	100.0
Mississippi	5.9	77.1	17.1	0.0	0.0	100.0
Missouri	5.2	58.3	36.5	0.0	0.0	100.0
Montana	1.8	53.6	30.0	14.7	0.0	100.0
Nebraska	1.6	48.8	49.7	0.0	0.0	100.0
Nevada	4.5	48.6	27.7	19.2	0.0	100.0
New Hampshire	2.2	45.1	47.4	5.2	0.1	100.0
New Jersey	2.3	58.4	39.3	0.0	0.0	100.0
New Mexico	2.4	49.4	33.6	13.7	0.9	100.0
New York	2.8	37.3	57.4	2.3	0.3	100.0
North Carolina	4.4	66.3	23.0	6.0	0.3	100.0
North Dakota	2.0	70.2	27.9	0.0	0.0	100.0
Ohio	2.1	50.8	30.4	16.3	0.4	100.0
Oklahoma	6.3	62.9	30.8	0.0	0.0	100.0
Oregon	1.7	37.4	45.5	15.1	0.4	100.0
Pennsylvania	6.0	63.8	26.6	3.2	0.5	100.0
Rhode Island	5.6	51.4	29.7	13.2	0.1	100.0
South Carolina	6.2	72.7	21.1	0.0	0.0	100.0

Table A-7. (Continued)

State	Teen Parents without a High School Diploma	Single Parents with a Child Under the Age of 6	Single Parents All Children Age 6 and Older	Two-Parent Family Not Receiving Federally Funded Child Care	Two-Parent Family Receiving Federally Funded Child Care	Totals
South Dakota	3.1	65.9	31.1	0.0	0.0	100.0
Tennessee	4.8	56.9	34.9	3.4	0.0	100.0
Texas	2.6	60.3	37.1	0.0	0.0	100.0
Utah	2.5	55.8	41.7	0.0	0.0	100.0
Vermont	3.0	29.0	44.0	24.0	0.0	100.0
Virginia	2.2	54.2	43.6	0.0	0.0	100.0
Washington	3.5	40.3	37.0	19.3	0.0	100.0
West Virginia	2.9	60.5	36.6	0.0	0.0	100.0
Wisconsin	7.7	56.9	30.3	4.8	0.3	100.0
Wyoming	0.7	57.6	36.3	5.4	0.0	100.0
Guam	3.7	0.0	64.1	31.7	0.6	100.0
Puerto Rico	4.6	49.8	45.6	0.0	0.0	100.0
Virgin Islands	8.9	73.0	18.1	0.0	0.0	100.0
Totals	2.9	48.7	38.0	10.2	0.1	100.0

Source: Congressional Research Service tabulations of the FY2011 TANF National Data Files.

Table A-8. TANF Sanctions and Sanction Rates by State: FY2011

State	Families on the Rolls		Families Leaving the Rolls		Combined Sanction Rate
	Number of Families anctioned	Percent Sanctioned	Number of Families Sanctioned	Percent Sanctioned	
Alabama	788	3.4%	451	24.6%	4.9%
Alaska	175	4.9	6	1.7	4.6
Arizona	258	1.4	0	0.0	1.3
Arkansas	531	6.5	3	0.6	6.2
California	43,952	7.3	6,986	13.9	7.8
Colorado	251	2.1	49	6.0	2.3
Connecticut	277	1.7	26	2.6	1.7
Delaware	97	1.8	148	59.2	4.2
District of Columbia	695	7.9	0	0.0	7.0
Florida	610	1.1	1,300	20.4	3.1
Georgia	122	0.6	14	1.3	0.6
Hawaii	0	0.0	227	33.1	2.3
Idaho	0	0.0	25	22.9	1.3
Illinois	1,243	4.4	0	0.0	4.0
Indiana	77	0.3	2,391	53.7	7.6
Iowa	0	0.0	23	1.5	0.1
Kansas	0	0.0	214	16.1	1.3
Kentucky	1,103	3.6	418	15.3	4.5
Louisiana	0	0.0	293	34.3	2.6
Maine	626	5.6	0	0.0	5.3
Maryland	9	0.0	888	25.6	3.1

Table A-8. (Continued)

State	Families on the Rolls		Families Leaving the Rolls		Combined Sanction Rate
	Number of Families anctioned	Percent Sanctioned	Number of Families Sanctioned	Percent Sanctioned	
Massachusetts	2,457	4.9	159	6.5	4.9
Michigan	0	0.0	1,513	28.2	2.1
Minnesota	1,013	4.4	116	5.0	4.4
Mississippi	23	0.2	374	39.8	3.1
Missouri	5,366	14.9	0	0.0	13.8
Montana	42	1.2	186	34.8	5.7
Nebraska	40	0.6	214	31.8	3.5
Nevada	0	0.0	123	12.5	1.0
New Hampshire	399	7.7	108	26.1	9.1
New Jersey	2,296	6.6	0	0.0	6.1
New Mexico	1,629	8.0	926	34.8	11.1
New York	5,563	4.5	0	0.0	4.2
North Carolina	18	0.1	864	43.3	3.5
North Dakota	202	11.1	35	15.8	11.6
Ohio	3	0.0	1,949	19.2	1.8
Oklahoma	1	0.0	453	38.9	4.5
Oregon	329	1.1	57	2.7	1.2
Pennsylvania	591	1.0	0	0.0	0.9
Rhode Island	217	3.3	71	8.2	3.9
South Carolina	17	0.1	469	27.8	2.5
South Dakota	43	1.3	119	38.0	4.5

State	Families on the Rolls		Families Leaving the Rolls		Combined Sanction Rate
	Number of Families anctioned	Percent Sanctioned	Number of Families Sanctioned	Percent Sanctioned	
Tennessee	0	0.0	1,453	31.5	2.2
Texas	0	0.0	551	13.3	1.0
Utah	0	0.0	138	24.9	2.1
Vermont	103	3.6	0	0.0	2.8
Virginia	0	0.0	191	9.9	0.5
Washington	2,730	4.4	292	5.0	4.4
West Virginia	411	4.0	149	16.8	5.0
Wisconsin	4,909	19.0	0	0.0	17.9
Wyoming	12	4.0	2	7.0	4.2
Guam	1	0.0	1	1.0	0.1
Puerto Rico	339	2.2	13	5.2	2.3
Virgin Islands	41	9.0	0	0.2	8.4
Totals	79,607	4.3	23,985	15.4	5.1

Source: Congressional Research Service tabulations of the FY2011 TANF National Data Files.

Notes: Combined sanctioned rate represents the sum of families on the rolls with benefits reduced because of sanctions and families with cases closed because of failure to work or comply with an activity requirement divided by the sum of total families on the rolls and the total number of families leaving the rolls in a month.

APPENDIX B. METHODOLOGICAL NOTES

TANF National Data Files

This report includes an analysis of work participation from the TANF National Data Files for FY2011. The national data files are based on data states are required to collect monthly and report to HHS on a quarterly basis based on Section 411 of the Social Security Act. These data provide information at the family and individual recipient levels, and include various demographic and economic data. Section 411 also requires that states report information required to compute TANF work participation rates, and HHS has specified that states report information on the average weekly hours of engagement in each of the 12 countable TANF work activities (see **Table 6**). States may report engagement in other activities not countable toward the official TANF work participation standards, but they are not required to do so.

The TANF National Data Files represent a sample of all TANF families and recipients receiving assistance. Thus, the estimates here are subject to sampling error. Additionally, there also may be nonsampling error associated with files if states miscoded some characteristics. There might also be some state-to-state variation in reporting practices that could affect data quality and the comparison of information from the files across states.

The TANF National Data Files differ slightly from the data used by HHS to compute the official TANF work participation rates. States may revise their data reports after submission to HHS. The publically available TANF National Data Files and the data used to compute official participation rates may reflect differing revised versions of the data.

Data Analysis

In conducting the data analysis for this report, certain decisions were made to try to reduce the possibility of including erroneously reported data. For example, the analysis excluded participation in an activity when 90 hours or more of participation per week were reported. Additionally, some recipients had implausible birth dates reported for them. No age was computed for these persons.

End Notes

[1] Prior to "mothers' pensions" (the first of which was enacted in 1911), the most common way care was provided for needy, dependent children was in institutions. Public sentiment began to shift toward the idea that children should be cared for in their own homes following the first White House Conference on Dependent Children in 1909. See Jo Anne B. Ross, *Fifty Years of Service to Children and Their Families*, Social Security Bulletin, October 1985/Vol. 48, No. 10., http://www.ssa.gov/policy

[2] U.S. Department of Labor, Children's Bureau, *Laws Relating to "Mothers' Pensions" in the United States, Denmark, and New Zealand,* Dependent Children Series, No. 1. Bureau Publication No. 7 (Washington, DC: Government Printing Office, 1914).

[3] Joanne L. Goodwin, *'Employable Mothers' and 'Suitable Work': A Re-Evaluation of Welfare and Wage-Earning for Women in the Twentieth-Century United States,* Journal of Social History, Vol. 29, No. 2 (Winter 1995), pp. 253-274.

[4] U.S. Department of Labor, Children's Bureau, *Laws Relating to "Mothers' Pensions" in the United States, Denmark, and New Zealand,* Dependent Children Series, No. 1. Bureau Publication No. 7 (Washington, DC: Government Printing Office, 1914).

[5] Ethel Cleland, *Pensions for Mothers*, The American Political Science Review, Vol. 7, No. 1 (February 1913), pp. 96- 98.

[6] Joanne L. Goodwin, *'Employable Mothers' and 'Suitable Work': A Re-Evaluation of Welfare and Wage-Earning for Women in the Twentieth-Century United States,* Journal of Social History, Vol. 29, No. 2 (Winter 1995), pp. 253-274.

[7] See the Report of the Committee on Ways and Means, U.S. House of Representatives, 74th Congress, 1st Session on H.R. 7260, printed April 5, 1935, http://www.ssa.gov/history /reports/35housereport.html

[8] See the Report of the Committee on Economic Security to the President, transmitted to the President on January 15, 1935.

[9] See the Report of the Committee on Ways and Means, U.S. House of Representatives, 74th Congress, 1st Session, on H.R. 7260, printed April 5, 1935, http://www.ssa.gov/history

[10] Studies of the characteristics of the cash assistance caseload have measured race and ethnicity differently over time, precluding a precise analysis of the change in the racial/ethnic makeup of the caseload. However, there is enough evidence to point to the changing racial and ethnic makeup of the caseload. The Social Security Administration published a report on changes in the ADC caseload from 1942 to 1948 in 16 states. Over this period, the percent of recipient children who were non-white grew from 21.4% to 30.2%. By 1956, 40% of the caseload was classified as nonwhite. In 1973, data on whether or not a recipient was Hispanic became available. In that year, it was reported that white non-Hispanic heads accounted for a minority (38%) of all AFDC families. Blacks headed 43% of all AFDC families and Hispanics headed 13.4% of all AFDC families in 1973. These data are from various reports showing the characteristics of AFDC families over the years.

[11] Joanne L. Goodwin, *'Employable Mothers' and 'Suitable Work': A Re-Evaluation of Welfare and Wage-Earning for Women in the Twentieth-Century United States,* Journal of Social History, Vol. 29, No. 2 (Winter 1995), p. 262

[12] Joanne L. Goodwin, *'Employable Mothers' and 'Suitable Work': A Re-Evaluation of Welfare and Wage-Earning for Women in the Twentieth-Century United States,* Journal of Social History, Vol. 29, No. 2 (Winter 1995), p. 262.

[13] Susan W. Blank and Barbara B. Blum, *A Brief History of Work Expectations for Welfare Mothers*, The Future of Children, Vol. 7, No. 1 (Spring 1997).

[14] Report of the Senate Finance Committee, U.S. Senate, 84th Congress, 2nd Session, on H.R. 7225, printed June 5, 1956.

[15] *Special Message to the Congress: Program for Economic Recovery and Growth*, Speech delivered by President John F. Kennedy, February 2, 1961, http://www.presidency.ucsb.edu /ws/?pid=8111#axzz1rH0u7Ceg.

[16] See P.L. 87-31 (H.R. 4884).

[17] *Special Message to the Congress on Public Welfare Programs,* President Kennedy, February 1, 1962, http://www.presidency.ucsb.edu/ws/?pid=8111#axzz1rH0u7Ceg.

[18] A concern at the time was that the program's benefits and eligibility standards discouraged marriage. The program was thus renamed to indicate that its purpose was to provide assistance to *families*. Susan W. Blank and Barbara B. Blum, *A Brief History of Work Expectations for Welfare Mothers*, The Future of Children, Vol. 7, No. 1 (Spring 1997).

[19] An enrollee would receive $30 a month while in training, plus an allowance for child care and other work-related expenses. If they became employed, the first $30 of earnings plus one-third of subsequent earnings would not be taken into account when calculating the family's AFDC grant.

[20] William J. Reid and Audrey D. Smith, *AFDC Mothers View the Work Incentive Program*, Social Service Review, Vol. 46, No. 3 (September 1972), pp. 347-362.

[21] *Job Opportunity and Basic Skills Training Program (JOBS)*, ChildTrends 2003, http://www.childtrends.org/ lifecourse/programs/JOBS.htm.

[22] Daniel Friedlander and Gary Burtless, *Five Years After: The Long-Term Effects of Welfare-to-Work Program,* Russell Sage Foundation, New York, 1995.

[23] Judith M. Gueron and Edward Pauly, *From Welfare to Work*, Russell Sage Foundation, New York, 1991.

[24] Robert Moffitt, "Incentive Effects of the U.S. Welfare System: A Review," *Journal of Economic Literature*, vol. 30, no. 1 (March 1992), pp. 1-61.

[25] Alicia H. Munnell, ei, *Lessons from the Income Maintenance Experiments, Proceedings from a Conference Held in September 1986*, Federal Reserve Bank of Boston, 1986.

[26] For a discussions of the welfare reform proposals offered during the Nixon Administration, see Vincent J. Burke and Vee Burke, *Nixon's Good Deed: Welfare Reform* (New York: Columbia University Press, 1974); and Daniel P. Moynihan, *The Politics of a Guaranteed Income, the Nixon Administration and the Family Assistance Plan* (New York: Vintage Books, 1973).

[27] Mary Jo Bane and David T. Ellwood, *Transitions from Welfare to Work*, Urban Systems and Engineering Inc., Cambridge, MA, 1983.

[28] David T. Ellwood, *Targeting "Would-Be" Long-Term Recipients of AFDC*, Mathematica Policy Research, Princeton, NJ, 1986.

[29] This section discusses the most influential studies of the pre 1996 period. It is based on more comprehensive reviews published in the 2000 and 2004 *GreenBooks* published by the House Ways and Means Committee.

[30] For a discussion of this research, as well as how randomized controlled experiments became the preferred methodology of welfare reform experiments, see Judith M. Gueron and Howard Rolston, *Fighting for Reliable Evidence* (New York: Russell Sage Foundation, 2013).

[31] Judith M. Gueron and Edward Pauly, *From Welfare to Work,* Russell Sage Foundation, New York, 1991; and Daniel Friedlander and Gary Burtless, *Five Years After. The Long-Term Effects of Welfare-to-Work Programs*, Russell Sage Foundation, New York, 1995.

[32] See Thomas Brock, David Butler, and David Long, *Unpaid Work Experience for Welfare Recipients: Findings and Lessons from MDRC Research*, MDRC, MDRC Working Papers, New York, NY, September 1993.

[33] James Riccio, Daniel Friedlander, and Stephen Freedman, *GAIN: Benefits, Costs, and Three-Year Impacts of a Welfare-to-Work Program. California's Greater Avenues for Independence Program*, Manpower Demonstration Research Corporation, New York, September 1994.

[34] U.S. Department of Health and Human Services and the U.S. Department of Education, *National Evaluation of Welfare-to-Work Strategies: How Effective are Different Welfare-to-Work Approaches? Five Year Adult and Child Impacts for Eleven Programs*, 2001.

[35] Johannes M. Bos, Susan Scrivener, and Jason Snipes, et al., *National Evaluation of Welfare-to-Work Strategies. Improving Basic Skills: the Effects of Adult Education on Welfare-to-Work Programs*, U.S. Department of Education and U.S. Department of Health and Human Services, 2002.

[36] The MFIP program was established under waivers granted under Section 1115 of the Social Security Act and a separate provision of what was then Food Stamp law. In addition, several states evaluated enhanced earnings disregards under Section 1115 of the Social Security Act, including Connecticut, Delaware, Florida, Vermont, and Virginia.

[37] For a synthesis of the research finding for these programs, see Gordon L. Berlin, *Encouraging Work, Reducing Poverty: The Impact of Work Incentive Programs*, MDRC, March 2000.

[38] Thomas Brock, Fred Doolittle, and Veronica Fellerath, et al., *Implementation of a Program to Reduce Poverty and Reform Welfare*, MDRC, October 1997.

[39] For a discussion of this restructuring of low-income assistance programs and federal spending trends on low-income aid, see CRS Report R41823, *Low-Income Assistance Programs: Trends in Federal Spending*, by Gene Falk.

[40] Gregory Acs, Pamela Loprest, and Tracy Roberts, *Final Synthesis Report of Findings from ASPE's "Leavers" Grants*, U.S. Department of Health and Human Services, Office of the Assistant Secretary for Planning and Evaluation, December 2001.

[41] U.S. Department of Health and Human Services, Office of Planning Research, and Evaluation, Administration for Children and Families, *Increasing Employment Stability and Earnings for Low-Wage Workers, Lessons from the Employment Retention and Advancement (ERA) Project*, OPRE Report 2012-19, April 2012.

[42] U.S. Department of Health and Human Services, Office of Planning, Research and Evaluation (OPRE), Administration for Children and Families, *What Strategies Work for the Hard-to-Employ? Final Results of the Hard-toEmploy Demonstration and Evaluation Project and Selected Sites from the Employment Retention and Advancement Project*, OPRE Report 2012-08, March 2012.

[43] The AFDC sanction was the removal of the noncomplying adult from the assistance unit, a reduction in the family's benefit.

[44] For a description of these waivers, see U.S. Department of Health and Human Services, Office of the Assistant Secretary for Planning and Evaluation, *Setting the Baseline: A Report on State Welfare Waivers*, June 1997, http://aspe.hhs.gov/hsp/isp/waiver2/title.htm.

[45] See CRS Report RL30785, *The Child Care and Development Block Grant: Background and Funding*, by Karen E. Lynch.

[46] Before October 1, 2006, all families without an adult recipient were excluded from the work participation rate calculation. The Deficit Reduction Act of 2005 (P.L. 109-171) required HHS to issue regulations to determine the circumstances under which a family with a non-recipient parent must be included in the work participation rate calculation. The HHS

regulations generally require that states *include* the following types of families without an adult recipient in the work participation rate calculation: (1) except for three months in a 12-month period, families subject to a sanction that removes the adult from the TANF assistance unit; and (2) families that reach state time limits that remove the adult from the TANF assistance unit but continue aid on behalf of the family's children.

[47] This is based on data from the U.S. Census Bureau. See detailed data tables at https://www.census.gov/hhes/ socdemo/education/data/cps/2011/tables.html.

[48] Such barriers were examined in Susan Hauan and Sara Douglas, *Potential Employment Liabilities Among TANF Recipients: A Synthesis of Data from Six State TANF Caseload Studies*, U.S. Department of Health and Human Services, Office of the Assistant Secretary for Planning and Evaluation, October 2004.

[49] CRS Report RL32748, *The Temporary Assistance for Needy Families (TANF) Block Grant: A Primer on TANF Financing and Federal Requirements*, by Gene Falk.

[50] See Gayle Hamilton, *The JOBS Evaluation: Monthly Participation Rates in Three Sites and Factors Affecting Participation Levels in Welfare-to-Work Programs*, MDRC, July 1995.

[51] For a discussion, see CRS Report R43634, *Temporary Assistance for Needy Families (TANF): Eligibility and Benefit Amounts in State TANF Cash Assistance Programs*, by Gene Falk.

[52] Before TANF, a family subject to sanction would generally find only the adult's portion of the grant reduced. Though support for work over the receipt of welfare had been a popular idea for decades, formal sanction policies first gained federal backing in 1988 with the implementation of the Family Support Act. The act stipulated that work-eligible individuals who failed to participate or refused to accept legitimate offers of employment would have sanctions levied against them. The amount of the sanction was set at the adult portion of the family's AFDC grant. It was not until the early 1990s, when the federal government began granting waivers of the AFDC rules—including the element regarding adult-only sanctions—that states began to impose full-family sanctions.

[53] U.S. Department of Health and Human Services, *Engagement in Additional Work Activities and Expenditures for Other Benefits and Services, April-June 2011, A TANF Report to Congress*, March 2012.

[54] These regulations are at 45 C.F.R. §261.43.

[55] The number of two-parent families that received federally funded child care is very small, and therefore is not shown on the figure.

[56] The number of two-parent families that received federally funded child care is small, so making reliable estimates for this sub group is problematic. Therefore, the figure shows hours for all two-parent families.

[57] U.S. Government Accountability Office, *Temporary Assistance for Needy Families. State Maintenance of Effort and Trends. Testimony Before the Subcommittee on Human Resources, Committee On Ways and Means, House of Representatives*, GAO-12-713T, May 17, 2012, p. 13.

[58] U.S. Department of Health and Human Services, "Reauthorization of the Temporary Assistance for Needy Families (TANF) Program; Final Rules," 73 *Federal Register* 67721-6828, February 5, 2008.

[59] CRS Report R42627, *Temporary Assistance for Needy Families (TANF): Welfare Waivers*, by Gene Falk.

[60] These regulations are at 45 C.F.R. §261.51.

[61] *Working Toward Independence: Maximize Self Sufficiency Through Work and Additional Constructive Activities.* February 2002, http://georgewbush-whitehouse.archives.gov/news /releases/2002/02/welfare-book-04.html

[62] The bills are H.R. 4737 (107th Congress), passed by the House on May 16, 2002; H.R. 4 (108th Congress), passed by the House on February 13, 2003; and S. 1932 (109th Congress), passed by the House on November 18, 2005.

[63] The bills approved by the Senate Finance Committee are H.R. 4 (108th Congress), as amended, reported on October 3, 2003; and S. 667 (109th Congress), ordered reported on March 9, 2005.

[64] Gayle Hamilton, *The JOBS Evaluation: Monthly Participation Rates in Three Sites and Factors Affecting Participation Levels in Welfare-to-Work Programs*, MDRC, July 1995.

[65] U.S. Department of Health and Human Services, *FY2015 Budget in Brief*, February 2014, p. 117.

[66] CRS Report RL33975, *Vulnerable Youth: Background and Policies*, by Adrienne L. Fernandes-Alcantara.

[67] See Appendix A in CRS Report RL33975, *Vulnerable Youth: Background and Policies*, by Adrienne L. FernandesAlcantara for age eligibility rules in programs for youths.

[68] A recent study examined trends in inequality in college entry and completion. The study concluded that there was increasing advantages for children who grew up in high-income families in terms of college entry, persistence, and completion. The increases in inequality in educational outcomes was driven primarily by women; Martha J. Bailey and Susan M. Dynarski, *Gains and Gaps: Changing Inequality in U.S. College Entry and Completion*, National Bureau of Economic Research, Working Paper 17633, Cambridge, MA, December 2011.

[69] U.S. Department of Health and Human Services, Office of Planning, Research, and Evaluation (OPRE), Administration for Children and Families, *Subsidizing Employment Opportunities for Low-Income Families. A Review of State Employment Programs Created Through the TANF Emergency Fund*, OPRE Report 2011-38, December 2011.

[70] U.S. Department of Health and Human Services, Office of Planning, Research, and Evaluation, Administration for Children and Families, *Career Pathways as a Framework for Program Design and Evaluation. A Working Paper from the Innovative Strategies for Increasing Self-Sufficiency (ISIS) Project*, OPRE Report 2012-30, May 2012.

[71] David Jenkins, Matthew Zeidenberg, and Gregory Kienzl, *Educational Outcomes of I-Best. Washington State Community and Technical College System's Integrated Basic Education and Skills Training Program: Findings from a Multivariate Analysis*, Community College Research Center, Teachers College, Columbia University, May 2009. Note that the I-Best model was also categorized as a career pathways program in the report cited above.

[72] Nancy Martin and Samuel Halperin, *Whatever It Takes, How Twelve Communities Are Reconnecting Out-of-School Youth*, American Youth Policy Forum, 2006.

[73] For example, see Reshma Patel and Lashawn Richburg-Hayes, *Performance-Based Scholarships. Emerging Findings from a National Demonstration*, MDRC, MDRC Policy Brief, May 2012. See also Colleen Sommo, Alexander K. Mayer, and Timothy Rudd, et al., *Commencement Day: Six-Year Effects of a Freshman Learning Community at Kingsborough Community College*, MDRC, July 2012.

[74] The TANF work participation standard is often called a "process" measure, one that measures program activity but is not in itself the desired outcome. That is, engagement in activities is to lead to an "outcome," which is placement in a job. However, because the TANF work participation rate counts those who do have jobs while remaining on the rolls, it is not in itself a pure process measure. See U.S. Department of Health and Human Services, Administration for Children and Families and the Assistant Secretary for Planning and

Evaluation, *Report on Alternative Outcome Measures*, December 2000, http://aspe.hhs.gov /HSP/alt-outcomes00/index.htm.

[75] For an overview of issues related to performance measurement in public programs, particularly public workforce programs, see *The Performance of Performance Standards*, ed. James J. Heckman, Carolyn J. Heinrich, Pascal Courty et al. (Kalamazoo, MI: W.E. Upjohn Institute for Employment Research, 2011).

[76] Gwyn Bevan and Christopher Hood, "What's Measured is What Matters: Targets and Gaming in the English Public Health Care System," *Public Administration*, vol. 84, no. 3 (August 2006), pp. 517-538, quoted in Heckman, et al., cited above.

[77] James J. Heckman, Carolyn J. Heinrich, and Jeffrey Smith, "Do Short-Run Performance Measures Predict Long-Run Impacts," *The Performance of Performance Standards*, ed. James J. Heckman, Carolyn J. Heinrich, Pascal Courty, et al. (Kalamazoo, MI: W.E. Upjohn Institute for Employment Research, 2011), pp. 273-303.

[78] CRS Report R41917, *Welfare, Work, and Poverty Status of Female-Headed Families with Children: 1987-2012*, by Thomas Gabe.

INDEX

C

D

E

I

J

K

L

M

R

S

Y